MW01116120

FIERCE HOPE

FIERCE HOPE

Walking through Pain with
the God of the Universe

CORRIE NAPIER

**MANUSCRIPTS
PRESS**

COPYRIGHT © 2024 CORRIE NAPIER
All rights reserved.

FIERCE HOPE

Walking through Pain with the God of the Universe

ISBN   979-8-88926-110-0 *Paperback*

979-8-88926-109-4 *eBook*

979-8-88926-111-7 *Hardcover*

Dedicated to my namesake, Corrie Ten Boom,
a champion of unwavering forgiveness and
a beacon of fierce hope to the world.

Hope is not tied to the preferred end to our suffering. Hope is being immersed in a reality that is greater than our suffering.

—KENT CARLSON

Contents

Author's Note

The Lord is close to the brokenhearted and saves those who are crushed in spirit.

—PSALM 34:18

On the darkest day of my life, in November of 2010, I never could have guessed the following weeks, months, and years would contain some of my most hope-filled moments. As I faced my pain and felt invited to walk through it with God rather than trying to escape from it or hide it, I experienced a transformation.

The fearful and condemning noise that had driven me was quieted, and I began tuning in more to what God was saying and doing. I felt guided on a path where I learned how to heal, forgive, and rebuild my identity. I also noticed a fierceness rising up in me—a fierceness to fight the despair trying to pull me down, a fierceness to boldly step out and follow my dreams previously hidden, and a fierceness to love and serve others with a capacity I did not previously have.

My "11-11 moments" are how I describe the times during my intense pain when I suddenly felt seen and intimately known by God. Like little touch points of heaven meeting Earth, they were beams of light piercing through the darkness of my pain-filled world. The more I experienced, the more I felt drawn to and immersed in this reality of the spiritual realm.

I feel compelled to write this book because so many of us experience intense pain in the world, and I don't think the comfort I received from God during those years was just for me. I think the reason I got so much of it was so I could share it with others like you.

Praise be to the God and Father of our Lord Jesus Christ, the Father of compassion and the God of all comfort, who comforts us in all our troubles, so that we can comfort those in any trouble with the comfort we ourselves receive from God.

—2 Corinthians 1:3–4[1]

This book is for anyone, but it's especially for those who…

- Have experienced a sudden, disorienting, life-altering type of pain in life.
- Are in the fire of pain now and find themselves asking, "Where is God in this?"
- Are struggling to reclaim their identity and sense of purpose in the midst of pain.

I tell you this with confidence: God is close, aware of the exact details of your circumstances, familiar with your pain, stronger and bigger than your crisis, and confident in His plan of redemption over you. I want to encourage you that in the fire of pain, your senses are actually sharpened to recognize God and the unseen spiritual realm. If you choose, you can engage with God in that place, allowing Him to refine you through this fire. Here in the fire, we learn to depend on Him instead of other things we've been clutching for comfort or using for escape—security blankets that can become our idols.

My prayer is that as you read you, will not only feel God's closeness but also recognize the beauty, good, and new life He is bringing out of the ashes of your situation. To paraphrase something one of my favorite speakers, Graham Cooke, says, "The size of the obstacle in front of us will be dwarfed by the opportunity released behind it."[2]

For me, the huge opportunity released behind my pain was the opportunity to participate in God's kingdom—His redemptive activity and plans on Earth. My "11-11 moments" led me to the exhilarating—and sometimes terrifying—experiences you'll read about, ones that helped show me who I was created to be.

What's in *your* heart to do? Who are *you* created to be?

As you read these pages, I invite you to discover what I did—a real and personal God who wants to walk with you through your pain and redeem it.

To give you fair warning, I talk a lot in the book about hearing or sensing messages from God (you'll see them marked *in bold italics*), noticing things like 11:11 on a clock, or feeling drawn to do things like pick up a crumpled-up piece of newspaper. I recognize all this can feel very ambiguous and strange, like following a "sign."

It is ambiguous. It is strange.

How do I know I'm having a conversation with the God of the Universe and not just a conversation with my own thoughts? How do I know I wasn't just making it all up and calling it God? The truth is, hearing God's voice is not something I can empirically prove. But it is something people experienced all throughout the Bible, like Jeremiah being told by God to go down to a potter's house,[3] Jacob seeing a vision of a ladder going to heaven,[4] and Joseph dreaming about his brothers' bundles of grain bowing down to his.[5]

I first heard God's voice at twelve years old when a vision came to my mind of Jesus rescuing me. I committed my life to Him, stepping forward in a faith that felt given to me that day—a faith that allowed me to feel true stillness and an inner knowing my Creator was "around" and knew me. I believe that in my small step of faith, I received His Spirit.

In John 16, Jesus talks about His Spirit coming to guide us into all truth.[6] In Romans 8, we learn this Spirit who dwells in us does not lead us into fear but is a spirit of adoption and belonging to the Creator of the Universe with whom we can have close, familiar relationship, calling Him "Abba" (Daddy).[7] Intimate friendship with God is what I needed most during my painful years, although if I'm honest, that took me a very long while to truly grasp.

People used to constantly ask me if I had hope my husband would return. I did, because I knew God's heart was to restore our marriage. However, the meaning of "hope" expanded for me during those years. I think Pastor Kent Carlson from my parents' home church said it best:

"Hope is not tied to the preferred end to our suffering. Hope is being immersed in a reality that is greater than our suffering."

Looking back, I see no better way to go through pain than to do it standing immersed in this closeness with God, learning to be fixated on Him more than on our desired outcome.

Welcome to the journey of *Fierce Hope*.

Disclaimer

This memoir is my truthful recollection of actual events that happened in my life, referenced from my extensive journal, voice memo, and email records. Some conversations have been recreated and supplemented and some events compressed. The names and details of most people have been changed to respect their privacy.

I have used prayerful discernment along with wisdom from others to include only those details I felt would be helpful in sharing my own story and in advancing the underlying message of fierce hope to readers of this book. My heart toward Chase remains one of forgiveness.

CHAPTER 1

A Minnow

Anyone who knew me as a child would have thought I had an idyllic childhood, and externally, I did. My internal world was a different story.

The second child of four, I grew up in the upper middle-class suburbia of Northern Virginia, on the outskirts of Washington, DC, for the full run of elementary and middle school. I wore pleated plaid skirts to school in a conservative Christian world. Most of my school memories took place in the ten classrooms lining the upper hallway of a Presbyterian church, a red-carpeted chapel room down the ramp at the end of the hallway, and a big empty parking lot out back that the twenty of us filled with joyful sounds of Double Dutch, kickball, and handclap rhymes.

Our brick house was a colonial style and stood stately and homey on the edge of a willow-lined cul-de-sac. On most days, a dozen or so neighborhood kids would join me and my brothers to race with our nets and fishing poles down to the ring of forest behind our cul-de-sac. Its green grass hills sloped down to a giant pond full of tadpoles, catfish, bullfrogs, and adventure. Summers consisted of lemonade stands, camping trips, Super Mario 3, and daily treks down to the community pool, where we trained hard with our teammates to rise in our division and crush our local team rivals.

I remember, as a very young child of about five years old, sitting alone in the far back row of our big silver Astro van, overhearing my mom having a hushed conversation with her friend Elaine, who was in the front seat next to her.

"I feel so devastated for Margaret..." my mom whispered. "Gosh, the stress of dealing with two kids who would so blatantly disregard all the values they were raised with."

"I know," Elaine replied.

My mom went on. "Just incident after incident at the school for both of them, and now for her son to be kicked off the swim team for the alcohol issue. So sad. Let's take a minute now to pray for them."

I listened in covert silence, and my little brain churned.

I never want my mom to be disappointed in me like she is in those older kids.

I thought for a minute and then felt a lightbulb go on.

You know, I could actually guarantee that. I know myself, and I've never made a bad choice like that. I know right from wrong, and I can decide right here and now to just always choose the right thing and never choose the wrong thing.

I was very pleased with my conclusion, completely unaware how this vow of perfectionism would wreak havoc on my inner world for decades to come. It was an open invitation to what I can only describe as a subtle white noise—an insidious cocktail of guilt, shame, condemnation, fear, and anxiety—that slipped into my mind and started to slowly infiltrate my thoughts.

This Noise became my constant companion yet proved as elusive as a minnow from my childhood pond—fleeing to the shadows when I tried to shine a light on the source of my inner unrest. To stay balanced, I took on the persona of "the good and perfect kid" and became extremely skilled at holding up this mask. I had to. It's who I was. When I started doing bad things, I had to grip it even tighter to try to block out the Noise.

I can't remember exactly how old I was, maybe seven or eight, when I was playing Barbies with my cousin and something in me wondered, *Could I get away with stealing her Barbie hairdryer?* It was a beautiful hot pink, tiny, plastic accessory, and I slipped it into my pocket when she was looking away then pretended it had gone missing. I don't know why I went through with it, but I did. I earnestly searched for it with her, and of course, she never suspected a thing. That was the first bad thing I remember willfully choosing to do, and it ate me alive inside. I had stolen. I wasn't perfect anymore, and I had no way to process it.

I found myself shoving the guilt down deep, and as I did, the Noise grew louder ever so slightly. I knew a part of me was "bad" now, and I would just have to live with it, punish myself for it, and resolve to work even harder to maintain my perfect image so no one would ever suspect or find me out. This seemed to work, in a way. All throughout elementary school, I followed the rules at home to please my parents, observed the teachers and studied the material carefully to always get As at school, and was well liked by my many friends. I was able to forget about my bad side most of the time as the Noise blended into the background.

To my dismay, however, more bad things started to pile up—lying to my mom, accidentally saying "that sucks" on the playground, cheating on a test, and even writing fake secret admirer notes to a classmate. When I did something, the Noise would surge up, and I would feel terrified someone would find out what I had done. Voices in my head would yell at me, a cacophony of accusations.

"You are bad, and you know it."
"You can't go back and change what you did. It's done."
"They're going to find out."
"You're going to jail."
"You're going to die."
"You don't deserve to stop and relax or have fun."
"Just do better. You could have done better."

The volume knob continued creeping up and up, despite my efforts to control it.

I was a faithful church-goer, of course. That is what good girls did, and it's what my family did anyway. If I had done fewer than five "quiet times" (prayer and Bible study) that week, my pulse would race during the part of my girls' small group at Sunday school when we had to go around and share "our number" with each other. I had to do better. I would do better next week.

I just had to try harder.

CHAPTER 2

Encountering God

"I want to tell you a true story," the speaker said from his podium on the stage, adjusting the microphone and looking out at all eight hundred of us middle school students.

I was twelve years old and sitting cross-legged with everyone else on the red-carpeted floor of a massive hotel banquet hall. We were all there at a church youth retreat in Virginia Beach, Virginia.

We listened with rapt attention to the detailed story, which took a full thirty or forty minutes for him to tell. It was about a teenaged girl who had run away from home, rebelled against her parents, and gotten into drugs and prostitution to pay her way. Her father had dropped everything to try to find her and bring her home, traveling from state to state over several months.

Every time the father had gotten close or gotten into contact with her, she rejected him and kept running, getting deeper and deeper into her addictions. Finally, he had gotten a strong lead and found himself scouring the hallways of a rickety two-story apartment building, looking room to room for his daughter. He peeked through a partially opened bedroom door and spied an emaciated, half-dressed woman on a bed in the corner—his daughter! He rushed to her and knelt down, throwing his coat around her as joyful tears streaked his face.

"You're alive! Oh, my daughter! I love you. Let's go home."

She struggled to lift her head, a faint gleam rising in her sunken eyes. "Daddy..." Relief was in her voice. "I'm ready."

At that moment, they heard the downstairs door burst open and heavy footsteps thudding up the stairs.

"Daddy! They're coming! They won't let me leave this place."

The dad sprang to action, lifting his daughter and running over to the open window then out onto the fire escape.

"Just go, my love. Run! I'll be right behind you."

A surge of adrenaline filled the girl, and she raced down the shaky metal stairs.

Pop! Pop! Pop!

Three shots rang out and stopped her cold, only long enough for her to look up in shock as her father's body slumped over the ledge of the window. Too scared to scream, her legs carried her the rest of the way down. She narrowly escaped to freedom, back home to recover and start a new life. Her dad had sacrificed his life for hers.

When the story finished, you could have heard a pin drop in the room. The speaker challenged all of us to get up without saying a word and file out to find a place in the building or on the beach to sit and have alone time with God. We all picked up our Bibles and journals and shuffled out in complete silence.

I found a spot outside in the sand under a palm tree lit up by a landscaping light. I heard the ocean waves pounding the shore about twenty yards in front of me, only the white caps glinting in the moonlight.

I opened my Bible and looked down. It was Psalm 40. As I began to read, the rushing sound of the waves faded and a quietness engulfed me—a sudden, deep quietness. My mind was still. I hadn't even been conscious of the volume knob before this moment, much less that it had been on full blast in my head. The Noise was gone in an instant, and I could hear the sound of my own breath.

I'm not alone, I thought, glancing around as I continued to breathe in then out. The stillness was like a loving blanket around me of total and complete acceptance, with no conditions. I knew I had struck gold.

It's You, my heart whispered. *You are God. You see me.*

Yes, I heard in my heart.

So this was Him, His presence, His peace. This was encounter. I experienced a shivering sensation of smallness.

He was here, watching, speaking, hearing my breath, hearing me read Psalm 40, word by word, phrase by phrase.

I waited patiently for the Lord; he turned to me and heard my cry. He lifted me out of the slimy pit, out of the mud and mire; he set my feet on a rock and gave me a firm place to stand. He put a new song in my mouth...

Blessed is the one who trusts in the Lord, who does not look to the proud, to those who turn aside to false gods...

I proclaim your saving acts in the great assembly; I do not seal my lips...

Do not withhold your mercy from me, Lord; may your love and faithfulness always protect me...

My sins have overtaken me, and I cannot see. Be pleased to save me, Lord...You are my help and my deliverer; you are my God, do not delay.

—*Psalm 40:1–3a, 4, 9a, 11, 12b, 13a, 17a*[1]

I blinked as I looked up from my Bible, and a picture appeared in my mind's eye—the father from the story, his head slumped over the window ledge. But then it lifted, slowly, and it was Jesus's face, beaten and bruised, his eyes piercing mine with light. "I love you."

I had to know this love, this stillness, Him. I had to stop at nothing to pursue a life running hard after the source of this sudden freedom from the Noise that had dominated my inner world.

So, You're real, God. You see me.

Yes.

You see everything I've done wrong.

Yes, and I forgive you.

"I don't care what it costs me!" I shouted into the wind, tears pouring down my face. "I want to live for You. I will not be ashamed of You. I accept You. Come into my life."

The rushing sea wind swirled around me, and I filled my lungs with it, letting it lift me up and pull me toward the thundering foamy blackness before me.

I reveled in this newfound closeness of a God I knew so much about but had never truly encountered. He knew me! The salty spray kissed my already salty cheeks as heaving sobs burst out of me from somewhere very deep inside my soul.

I remember walking back to my hotel room afterward, and my roommates asked how my time had been out on the beach.

"I think I just felt the Holy Spirit," I said in a bit of a daze without a chance to think.

Right then, another round of sobs gushed out of me, and one of my friends, Sarah, rushed over to hug me. I wept openly on her shoulder for almost a full minute; sobs from that same deep place in my soul, a place where so much had been hiding—afraid, guilty, and shameful. The release of it was a completely new feeling, a new freedom. I had never cried like that in front of people.

How strange, I remember thinking. *I don't care at all what my friends are thinking of me right now.*

I was changed that trip. I started thinking about God all the time, talking to Him, and writing prayers in my journal.

I wanted more encounters with Him. And they did happen throughout middle school with that same characteristic stillness. The Noise would disappear for a bit but would then find a way to gradually turn the volume knob back up in my head while causing me to nearly forget about its existence.

For the start of high school, my dad had taken a new job in business development and moved our family from Northern Virginia to Hong Kong. I attended a diverse international school on the south side of Hong Kong island, which massively expanded my worldview and interest in other cultures. For these formative two years abroad, I was also part of a nondenominational youth group called Saturday Night Alive and attended gatherings where I learned to "soak" in the presence of God. In that atmosphere of music, worship, and prayer, I would feel the stillness again, my Creator reminding me I didn't need to be perfect. I loved it.

Other than at youth group, I primarily reached out to God when I was making big decisions or when I needed something from Him. Temporary clarity and relief would come in those instances, but it was me and the Noise in my mind for the rest of the time. I longed for more stillness with God—the place full of love and absent of condemnation—but it always seemed just out of reach.

I just need to get through this... do this... check this off my list... see this person... get to the place I should be... then I'll come to You, God, for that encounter. Then I'll come to You.

Then. Then. The harder I tried to get to some "perfect" place to earn my encounter with God, the more I felt trapped in the Noise, stuck in this loud, fearful, self-focused cycle that kept reinforcing the perfectionism lie. It seemed clear in my mind it was my fault I wasn't closer to God, and I relentlessly punished myself for it. As I did, I found myself struggling to be present, scattered in my thoughts, second-guessing myself in most decisions, and addicted to pleasing others.

How do I break free of this, God?

We moved from Hong Kong back to the US in 1998, and I spent my final two years of high school at a huge public school in northern California. Toward the end of my senior year, I got a gift from God I thought was the answer— someone to help me break the cycle and quiet the Noise.

His name was Chase.

CHAPTER 3

Godsend

"He's a junior," my tour guide said, pointing to an attractive college guy singing in the second to last row. "And he goes to that church you said you wanted to check out."

I was a bright-eyed seventeen-year-old high school senior on a college campus tour, and my private tour guide was dropping me off at the final stop—to observe the concert choir rehearsal.

"You should talk to him afterward," she suggested as she headed out for her next tour.

"Thanks. I will," I replied.

Up to this point, I had not gotten a great impression of the college but had decided to be open-minded and give it one final chance that day before my flight back home to northern California later in the evening.

I sat alone behind the choir director, who was positioned in the front corner of the room facing four risers of about sixty college students. Their eyes were focused with quiet expectation on their sheet music as they waited for the cue from the director. Then, with the flick of his hand, the room came suddenly alive, reverberating with the stunning harmonies of a beautiful and haunting Latin piece, *Agnus Dei*.

The junior guy my tour guide had pointed out earlier was singing in the tenor section. I noticed his wave of brownish blond hair, piercing blue eyes, and overall clean-cut appearance. He was very attractive, but I was trying not to dwell on this since I had a boyfriend. Plus, this guy was in college, and I was only a high schooler.

After the director dismissed the class, I waded through the sea of departing students to make my approach. He was taller than I thought.

"Hi. You're Chase, right?"

"Yep." He nodded.

"I'm Corrie. Just touring today, and my guide suggested I meet you to ask you some questions about your church. Do you happen to have a minute?"

His face lit up as he checked his watch. "Sure. Actually, I have a break now between classes, and it's going to take more than a minute to tell you about the church. It's really amazing. You want to go have a chat in the amphitheater? It's right around the corner."

"Sure. Wow, thanks so much," I replied.

As we sat in the sun, Chase started sharing.

"God is doing so much at our church and on this campus. He's really speaking to people, and we're learning how to hear Him. You see the chapel right there? One of our leaders got a vision of the presence of God falling from heaven, like a white fire, right down onto it then spreading over the campus."

I was captivated as he continued.

"Being part of this community has been so transformational for me. We have an awesome young adults group with such powerful times of worship. We just get lost in it, and people start writing new songs and just flowing. I assume you sing?" he asked.

"Yeah, I sing on the worship team at my youth group, in choir, and am also part of an a cappella group at my high school. It's actually really refreshing to hear you talk about your church and everything God is doing on campus because no one I've met here until now has given any indication of that. And now I'm about to leave!"

"Oh man," he said. "You should come back on a weekend and check out the church. I can introduce you around to my friends and the leaders. You really need to check it out."

I felt an immediate chemistry with Chase, just an ease of being around him and a shared spiritual hunger. I took him up on his suggestion and flew back down to campus a few weeks later. After attending an afternoon worship service then spending the whole evening with Chase and his friends,

I knew. These were my people. This was my church. This was my school.

I signed my acceptance letter and held it up in front of everyone. "I'm coming to school here!" I yelled.

They all cheered.

I remember my stomach fluttering as I wrote Chase an email after my high school graduation, starting it with "Hey, Godsend..." I told him how impactful meeting him had been, thanking him for taking so much time to connect me with his group of friends.

"No problem," he responded. He also shared with me that because the young adults group was getting so big, he and a few others would be leading a new group that fall with just the college students.

"Do you want to be on our worship team for the new group?" he asked.

"Absolutely!" I replied. I was thrilled to get involved right away.

We exchanged a couple more emails over the summer, but I was busy getting ready for college and was in the midst of a breakup with my high school boyfriend.

Arriving to college that fall was like a dream. I felt almost immediately at home. The first time I saw Chase again in person, he was sitting outside the church, casually playing a guitar. His fingers flew across the strings so naturally. My heart skipped a beat.

"You play guitar too?" I exclaimed. "I had no idea!"

"Hey! Welcome back, stranger." He turned to me and smiled and then got up to give me a hug.

It was exhilarating to sing backup with Chase on the worship team of the new college group and lead others together. The chemistry from our first meeting was still there and only getting stronger, and I found myself creating reasons to get to church early or to linger afterward to help him with the music equipment.

Of course, I wrote the whole thing off as an impossible little crush—he was so much older—but after a month or so, I started getting some flirty vibes from him as well. I realized we were spending a lot of time together, and the whole dynamic was a bit distracting during worship practice. So, when an acquaintance told me he had a girlfriend, my stomach dropped, and I marched over to his apartment on campus that night to confront him.

"Can we talk for a sec?"

"Sure," he said, standing in the doorway.

Gosh, those blue eyes, I thought. *Stop it, Corrie. He has a girlfriend. Get to it.*

"Chase, I have loved being on the worship team with you, and want to continue that…"

I hesitated.

"It's just that… as your sister in Christ… I'm a bit confused because I know you have a girlfriend, and I've been getting some mixed messages from you. I just want to be really careful, and clear, and focused, because we are leading worship together, and that is a serious…"

"I don't have a girlfriend," he interrupted. "Whoever told you that must not have known we broke up weeks ago."

"Oh," I said, blushing.

"Can I tell you something else?" he asked.

"Okay," I answered.

"Corrie, I've been sending you mixed messages because… I'm crazy about you."

My eyes widened. "*What?*" My thoughts were scrambled, but words just came out. "I'm crazy about you too."

He came toward me and gently wrapped his arms around me. We stood there for a minute, hearts pounding, adjusting to this new reality.

I laughed. "Whoa, this was not what I was expecting to happen tonight."

"I'm glad it did," he said. "But I want to take you out on a proper first date as well."

"That sounds great," I said.

A few days later, we grabbed sandwiches and dulce de leche ice cream from the grocery store and headed to the beach for a picnic. We talked and laughed for hours, long after the sun had disappeared over the horizon.

Chase is so special. I can't believe this is happening!

It was an unlikely relationship with our age difference, but we found a unique place amid our mixed-age group of friends at the church. On campus, Chase was a well-known, respected, and charismatic leader, and I remember more than a few people raising their eyebrows when they found out I was his girlfriend.

"Whoa, you're dating Chase? Lucky girl. How did you pull that off? He is a hot ticket on campus and such a quality guy."

I adored Chase. I looked up to him and found myself trusting him, sometimes even more than I trusted myself. We were on the same page about most things and basically "did everything right" by Christian standards. Our relationship was fun, free, and full of spiritual experiences with our dynamic community. Chase was always making me laugh with his random accents, impressions, and silliness.

His carefree silliness combined with his spiritual maturity was such a rare find. I remember telling him about my internal struggle with the fearful and condemning Noise and my desire to connect more deeply with God. His encouraging response propelled me forward in my relationship with God.

"You already hear from God, Corrie. You just need to trust it's His voice," he told me. "I also encourage you to try processing these feelings directly with Him."

Chase and I practiced listening to God together, praying for our friends as well as our families. I started reading my Bible more and noting in my journal what I sensed I was hearing from God. I also started paying more attention to dreams.

I remember one day, alone in my dorm room, I started singing lines of a song I'd never heard before. I sensed it was a song from God because it brought this immediate peace, like a mute button to the destructive Noise.

Another day when I was driving, I saw a Ryder truck with the slogan "Together, we'll ride on into the future." I sensed these words were for me in that moment, reassurance from God that He was with me. This felt confirmed when a rainbow appeared across the sky in front of me while a song came on the radio with a line about a girl being wonderful like a rainbow on a cloud!

Wow, God. So You don't just see me; You have things to say to me.

It felt like a veil was being lifted, and I started to hear from God more and more.

CHAPTER 4

Eleven

"You're so behind."
"You're never going to get everything done."
"You haven't been disciplined enough."
"You shouldn't be feeling this anxious."

I was alone in the car with my thoughts. They were loud and crashing in on me, especially without a fun boyfriend to help drown them out. It was a long weekend during my college years, and I was driving the six hours from Los Angeles back home to northern California. I had been very busy with schoolwork and hadn't connected with God in a while.

I remember crying and saying out loud, "God, are You there? I need You. I feel so far from You."

Right then, my car's odometer caught my attention. I noticed the number was 111,110, with the zero changing at that very moment to a one.

I gasped—111,111 miles.

The perfect number seemed to stare back at me as a rush of peace hit my senses like a blast of refreshing wind. I experienced that same inner knowing of being seen I'd felt years ago at twelve years old on the beach.

You're here, God.

Yes.

That's all I needed—to be seen and known by the living God. I took a deep breath as tears streamed down my face.

I'm sorry I've been so distant. Thank You for being with me.

I'm always here with you.

The stillness that stopped the Noise was there in that moment, as well as the wonderful sense of smallness and the sense of being completely loved, seen, and accepted.

From that day on, I started noticing elevens—my special number, a signpost the God of the Universe knew me and was around. During many moments, I saw a clock reading 11:11, and when I did, I would feel a strong sense of His peace and presence. Sometimes, when I was praying and seeking answers about something, I would see an eleven and hear:

I see you. I know you. I'm here.

The experience of God's presence alone would bring the stillness and perspective I needed to flow. With whatever question I was asking Him, I would either know what to do in the situation I was facing or it would fade into unimportant oblivion.

When this happened, I longed to stay in that place of peace, but it always felt elusive. I came to believe a place of sustained peace and closeness with God was not possible or realistic.

Also, I had Chase, who became my primary support. He always had the right thing to say and had a knack for making me feel better. I slowly began to rely on him for this, even when we did our second year of dating long distance when I studied abroad in South America. He had gotten a job at our college after he graduated, so when I returned, I was able to see him all the time. Despite my spiritual growth during college, I continued to be an adoring fan of my "much older" and "much wiser" boyfriend.

Chase always seemed to have things together and take challenges in stride. For example, in the middle of my college years, when his parents suddenly divorced, he was clearly devastated and hurt for a while but was able to bounce back. Whenever I asked him about it, he always said he was okay and working through it with God.

Another challenge came up around the same time. Our church split due to some leadership issues, and we all had to regroup. Despite being extremely upset and voicing some concerns about how church was done in general, Chase seemed to shift gears well and started coleading the college group out of his house for a while until we all got settled in other churches. His ability to press forward despite doubts felt like a strength of resiliency, at least at the time.

Chase was truly everything I had hoped for and more. I didn't feel like I had to perform for him or try to be perfect.

I could just be myself, though my sense of self was wrapped up more and more in being his girlfriend.

In November of my senior year of college, we had both been super busy, and he asked if I wanted to head to the beach that night to just unwind, worship, pray, and connect.

"Sounds amazing," I told him.

He brought his guitar out to the sand, along with a couple of blankets since it was quite chilly, even for California. He played a few songs, and we lifted our voices to heaven, breathing in the ocean air as the setting sun painted the sky with a stunning array of pinks, oranges, and purples. I felt a calm come over me, a quietness I knew well. I got up to take a little solo walk to stretch my legs and drink in the beauty.

You're here, God.

Yes.

I love Chase. Everything about being with him just helps me feel Your peace, free from the fear and condemnation I normally deal with.

I paused.

I want to marry him.

The waves were gentle that night, breaking on the shore in a steady rhythm that soothed my soul. I remember the thought that came next.

Gosh, this is it. This is the moment I will tell Chase about later if he ever asks me to marry him. This is the moment I knew. I have to remember to tell him.

I squished my toes into the cool sand as I walked back to the blanket. Chase was fiddling around on the guitar and looked up.

"Hey, did I tell you I wrote a third verse to that worship song I wrote last year?" he asked.

"I don't think so," I replied.

He started playing and singing, and I joined to fill in harmony, as I always did. It was called "Love of My Life," and we had sung it together many times at the college group. When he started the third verse, I stopped short.

This was not a third verse to God. He was singing this verse directly to me. It was about me. We stared into each other's eyes as tears streamed down both of our faces.

This is the moment, God? You knew this was going to happen! I literally only felt ready to say yes about three minutes ago!

Chase wiped his eyes as he reached back to grab a small box, and then he knelt in the sand. "Will you marry me?"

As I opened the box, an automatic light flashed on, illuminating a dazzling diamond ring. We both laughed at the sudden intensity of light bursting into the growing darkness.

"Yes, of course I will." I fell forward to embrace my beloved Chase.

We're getting married!

Eight months later, during the summer after I graduated college, Chase became my husband.

Our wedding was indeed full of God's peace and such joy! People told us afterward they had never been to a wedding so full of the presence of God.

During the ceremony, Chase and I led worship together with a beautiful song about Jesus being enough. A slide show displayed pictures from both of our childhoods up through the four years of our relationship. Then our bridal party came and laid hands on us to pray. As they did, I remember a stirring in my spirit as I felt the mystery of oneness with the incredible guy standing across from me. I breathed out.

You're here, God.

Yes.

Chase and I had both shared the conviction to save sex for marriage, and as each other's firsts, we laughed a lot as we figured things out on our beautiful honeymoon in Canada and savored the unity of our new marriage.

After two wonderful years and a lot of prayer, we decided to make a leap and move overseas to China. We felt drawn to go on an adventure and experience God in the context of a new culture.

Our close friend, Colton, had forged a path in Shanghai and raved about it so much that we took an initial short trip there to see it for ourselves. We fell in love with the city, and Colton was elated we would be joining him there. Several months later when we arrived, he helped us find a fantastic three-bedroom apartment, enroll in language school, and get connected to his dynamic international church community.

Life in China was a constant adventure. We studied Chinese for two years then both landed dream jobs in education. I was head of admissions at a bilingual international school for kids from preschool to high school. Chase was the founding director of a new study abroad program for American college students. We were very involved at the international church, joined the worship team, and started coleading Bible studies and Alpha groups.

Our integration into our new faith community and our explosion of personal growth were so exciting I felt like I was growing spiritually when I was actually quite stagnant. I didn't notice Chase was initiating prayer and time with God less and less.

Even though I was still having conversations with God, I was going back to my old habit of turning to Him only when I needed help. My life was so full of other things, especially Chase, who was now my easy go-to source of affection and the one I constantly looked to for validation, like a security blanket.

I remember in the mornings before I got out of bed, I got into the daily habit of asking Chase, "Am I okay?"

He would always answer, "Yes, love. You're okay."

By 2010, life in Shanghai as I experienced it was vibrant, fast-paced, dynamic, and fun. The six years since our wedding had seemed mostly idyllic.

Little did I know that overhearing a single phone call would bring my idyllic world crashing down.

CHAPTER 5

The Pain Begins

By the time I got home that night, it was after 11:00 p.m. I decided to take the stairs—thirteen floors up—one chalky concrete step at a time, in our apartment building in Shanghai. Images of the caring and concerned faces of my closest friends floated through my mind as I thought about the small group gathering I had just attended at the apartment of my close friends, Leanna and James, across the street—a place where, yet again, I cried tears of frustration, loneliness, and longing.

My husband, Chase, was in crisis: angry all the time, standoffish, frustrated, his blue eyes cold and distant. I didn't know why. He had spent the month of July back in the States starting a correspondence PhD program in higher education, and he told me when he returned to our home in Shanghai that while away, some big questions had stirred up inside himself. In college, he had studied philosophy and religion and had always been a deep thinker.

He explained how the initial phase of the PhD program involved examining his personal epistemological views—his approach to knowledge and truth—and deeply reflecting about how they impacted his own biases and objectives as a researcher. I tried digging into the big questions he was grappling with about absolute truth and how we as imperfect humans construct meaning in a fallen world, but he kept telling me he just needed space and time to think—alone. He would apologize and say he felt conflicted, frustrated, and upset, and he just needed to get to the bottom of it.

As the accommodating person I was, I gave him his space, as much as he needed—whatever I could do in an attempt to get my husband back as soon as possible.

I suffered on my own, week after week—crying daily and wondering when the storm would blow over, when his Xbox would finally be shut off, and when his cigars and cigarettes "to think" would be smothered out. It was only a matter of time, of course. We had what I considered a great marriage, and Chase was an extremely intelligent, capable guy. Of course starting a PhD would stir up deep questions. I just had to grit my teeth, cling to the side of the ship, and wait for the waves to subside. But it was hard, even though he said it had nothing to do with me.

Where I normally saw room-warming charisma and sharp hilarious wit, I now saw only hollow light and laughter coming from the one I loved. He was emotionally absent and seemed incapable of giving. He kept to himself, and I stayed busy at work, crying with my friends and waiting it out… waiting it out… trying not to think too seriously about it… nursing my wounds and trying to be as supportive of Chase as I could.

But life was so loud—so busy and so loud. The Noise was on full blast. Even when he expressed his anguish to me in some ways—"Corrie, you really want to know how I feel? I feel like I want to throw myself off this building!"—I had little to offer other than to continue to accommodate him. I was very concerned about Chase, but I knew he was a confident person and could sort it out with God the way he always had with other challenges in the past.

I needed him to sort it out soon. It was already November, and I wanted my husband back for the comfort, love, and affection I craved.

Then that night, instead of the storm blowing over, lightning struck.

As I entered our apartment and hung up my coat, I heard the muffled but distinct sound of Chase laughing and talking excitedly, his voice animated and full of life. I knew his good friend, Andy, who always made him laugh, had been trying to reach him for weeks.

Thank You, God! Andy must be on the phone cheering him up. Ahh! This is the breakthrough I've been waiting for. Finally! Chase is back to his old self.

Chase was out on the balcony, a glass door separating me from him physically but not masking the sound or tone of his voice. How it warmed my heart to hear his genuine laugh again. I tapped on the glass to announce my arrival, and he looked at me, holding up one finger to indicate he was in the middle of the call.

Good! I thought. *Take your time. I'll get ready for bed.*

I hummed to myself, thinking how wonderful it would be to finally connect with my husband again—emotionally, physically, and spiritually. The dark cloud over the previous three months had been rough.

I finished brushing my teeth and came back out to the living room. He was still out on the balcony. I wondered what he was talking to Andy about, and I needed to get to bed soon. My curiosity piqued, and I sat still to listen in for a minute. Then I froze, his words entering my consciousness but not my reality.

"Rachel, I love you so much. If I could, I would fly over right now to hold you. I love you so much, so much... Telling Corrie... We need to think about your kids... And I really want to be a father."

Lines of a play. He must be rehearsing lines of a play. Maybe with his sister, who is an actress? Chase must be helping her with her lines.

Mechanically, on my cue in the play, I walked over to the glass door and tapped again, this time cracking it open.

"Chase, I really need to go to bed. Can you please wrap it up so you can tuck me in?"

The actor's answer: "Yes. Sorry, it's my boss on the phone. We've had some issues, and I'm just sorting them out. I'll be in soon."

A lie. Chase just lied to me.

My heart pounded with each step toward the bedroom door.

Do I call Leanna? Do I pretend I didn't hear what I just heard and tell Leanna so I know what to do? What do I do? Oh, God! Of course this isn't an affair. It's Chase. He adores me.

I heard the scraping sound of the opening balcony door and his footsteps up the stairs. Hollow words hit me as I sat on the bed and stared up at the face of my husband.

"Sorry, love," he said. "There were some students in the program who got drunk, and there has been drama with the parents. I had to explain everything to my boss and calm down the parents."

Despite the pounding in my chest, I heard calm words come out of my mouth.

"Chase, I know you were not talking to your boss. Who is Rachel, and why do you love her?"

His eyes closed, and he took a deep breath, half smiling. Or was it a grimace? He sat down on the bed, and I sat cross-legged, facing him, intent, and fully awake. He was calm too. He sighed again then looked up.

"Rachel is a woman from my PhD program. I met her in the US in July."

The story tumbled out, a really strange scene from a fictional movie. A movie about other people's lives. Other people who have affairs. People who are not happily married to the love of their life. People who did not receive multiple confirmations that God had brought them together. People who were not right for each other. A movie about those people. Not about me and Chase.

Could someone please turn off this movie? I have work tomorrow. It's late.

But there was no remote.

The move kept playing—this fictional Chase sharing about the new love of his life. A new color in the rainbow he didn't know existed before. Like he and Rachel were married in a previous life and just "knew" each other when they met, as if remembering. That it felt like he had no choice but to connect with her, be with her. That he loved her very much… very much. That their connection had made him come alive artistically, intellectually, and spiritually; had opened up the door to a room in his heart he didn't know was there.

They had felt compelled to open that door for each other. The choice in their minds had been between causing some pain now to those around them by being together or causing more pain later if they denied this door was there.

Of course he had been planning to tell me, he said, but was conflicted about what to do next, how to handle all these new things, and how to tell me. He had to explore everything more first, to figure out how this woman could exist, especially because she was married and the mother of two small children.

I remembered he had sought out a counselor a few weeks prior… Yes, the counselor had given him a book about affairs and had encouraged him to talk to me about things sooner rather than later.

I remembered his sudden decision to go cold turkey vegetarian when he got back from the States… Yes, Rachel had "inspired" him.

Then the dreaded question: Had they slept together? Yes, they had "made love." They had even prayed together.

What?

A stranger… A week after meeting her… I sucked in my breath and paused for a moment, looking down at my trembling hands and feeling the sting of the first tears. Just a few because this was not really happening.

This is not real. It's just so strange to hear him say "made love" and "love her very much." My Chase only loves me very much. And only makes love to me. Has only ever made love to me.

Tears just came out. These strange, strange words of this story.

Suddenly, I coughed out, "Wait a minute."

Psalm 46—the passage that had grabbed my attention months ago. At the time, I hadn't known why, but now it suddenly made sense, and the verses came surging up like bubbles in water to the surface of my consciousness. As surreal as everything was, I found myself with enough presence of mind to get off the bed and grab my Bible, opening up to Psalm 46.

"I think I need to read this."

Chase shrugged. "Okay."

My voice trembled as I read.

God is our refuge and strength, an ever-present help in trouble. Therefore we will not fear, though the earth give way and the mountains fall into the heart of the sea, though its waters roar and foam and the mountains quake with their surging. There is a river whose streams make glad the city of God, the holy place where the Most High dwells…

[The Lord] says 'Be still, and know that I am God; I will be exalted among the nations, I will be exalted in the earth.' The Lord Almighty is with us; the God of Jacob is our fortress."
                                            —*Psalm 46:1–4, 10–11*[1]

I finished reading and grabbed his hands. "Can we pray?"

"Okay," he said again, the same hollow look on his face.

I closed my eyes.

"God, we come to You knowing You're here. Whatever happens from this point, we trust You and need You and invite You in to help. We need Your help. Amen."

I paused, blinking open my eyes.

Then more questions poured out in a steady flow. "Does Rachel's husband know? Are they still together? How often have you been talking to her?"

Chase kept calmly answering, but his words had nowhere to land in me, nowhere to register, as if I were flipping through language settings on my TV, trying to find one I could understand. *Does not compute. Does not compute.*

Chase? Chase! Where are you?
Someone here is hurting me, and I need you.
I need you to hold me. Explain this to me, please, Chase. Chase?
Where are you? Who is this person?
Chase, I know you. You know me.
Hold me, Chase. Who is this person I'm talking to?
I don't understand anything he's saying. Please hold me.
Please explain this to me. What is happening?
What is happening?

This Chase was calm, sighing deeply as he answered my questions one by one, sitting there on the bed across from me, looking down. But not in shame. Not a shred of remorse. Instead… What was this eerie confidence? He spoke with authority like a parent patiently explaining very complicated things to a child, anticipating each question I would ask. He did not expect me to understand the "depth of the truths" he had stumbled upon with Rachel. They were even too deep for him in some ways, and that was the beautiful mystery of it. He was awakened and alive, intoxicated by this feeling, this woman, this new exploration and embracing of his "true self."

"Corrie, I've read a lot about affairs, and this does not fit into any normal category. I know, of course, what people will say—that I'm either totally crazy or totally deceived. But I'm telling you sincerely, I'm not either one. I've looked at it from every angle, and I'm trying to understand it. That's why I'm in counseling. And I think you should be too. It would be good for you to talk through things with someone."

I was sobbing now. My Chase. He was passionate, alive in this new way. Confident. How? These amazing things he shared about his "true" self, his desires. This sense of being "unlocked." I intensely wanted to understand this new alive Chase. Had he really done these things? How could this be?

If this wasn't an affair, what was it? Was Rachel really supposed to be in his life? Was he supposed to stay married to me and stay connected to her somehow? Of course, it couldn't be a real affair. Chase loved me. Chase was my husband. So what was it?

Confusion drew me into exhaustion, and at 3:30 a.m., I curled into a ball on my side of the bed and quietly shook. I was cold and gasping for air.

Oh God, oh God, oh God!

"Chase, can you please hold me?" I whimpered.

It just came out, like I was on autopilot. Chase always tucked me in if I went to bed before him. He hesitated and furrowed his brow.

"Okay…" He lay behind me on the bed with one arm over and around me. I clutched his hand and felt the assurance of his warmth against me.

Then "she" was there in my mind all of a sudden: him with "her"; him being intimate with "her," this mother of two. I dry heaved and threw his arm off me, repulsed and terrified. My security blanket had become like icy steel, so cold it burned.

Oh God, oh God, oh God.

He moved over and got up. "I think it's best if I sleep in the guest room."

I didn't answer. I was frozen as I heard the door close and then his footsteps going back down the stairs.

My mind was racing. More images of him with her, him with her, him with her. More questions. The pounding of his answers, his words, on my consciousness, beginning a torment. *Crash, crash, crash.*

Make it stop! Chase, where are you? Where are you?

My mind was spinning, spiraling into a black abyss.

What if I lose Chase? I would die. He is my everything. How could he be saying these things about God? Could they be true? Have I misunderstood everything about God? Chase seems so confident and inspired. What could I be missing?

This was the beginning of my pain, a state of utter shock—not anger, just desperation, confusion, and torment. I was so utterly unprepared for this crisis.

Or was I?

Psalm 46 had come right to my mind in the midst of that traumatic moment, as well as the sense to grab Chase's hands and pray. It was a simple prayer, a desperate cry for help. But it's exactly what was needed, and God began to answer it right away.

I woke up the next morning and called in sick.

CHAPTER 6

The Preparation

Five months before overhearing that phone call, on June 21, 2010, I wrote in my journal:

"God, I want to hide with You, in the shelter of Your wings—there, the enemy doesn't know where I am... Teach me more about the spirit realm. I'm caught up in lies. Can't function well."

A few days later, I was listening to a sermon, and the pastor suggested asking God to highlight a section in the Bible to focus on, as opposed to randomly flipping through pages and reading, which is what I tended to do. So I took a moment to pray.

God, what do You want me to focus on in the Bible?

I paused to listen.

Psalm 46.

The scripture reference jumped to my mind, and I opened to it.

God is our refuge and strength, an ever-present help in trouble. Therefore we will not fear, though the earth give way and the mountains fall into the heart of the sea, though its waters roar and foam and the mountains quake with their surging...

[The Lord] says 'Be still, and know that I am God; I will be exalted among the nations, I will be exalted in the earth.'
—Psalm 46:1–3, 10[1]

My heart stirred. This was it! My verses for the coming days... weeks? Months? I wasn't sure. How refreshing to know, though, that one chapter was all I needed to focus on until God stirred me to go elsewhere. I read it aloud, wrote it out by hand, and memorized the first few verses.

Then came July 1, 2010, a day I had dedicated to fasting and prayer. I had a feeling from a prayer session the previous year with a friend that July 2010 would be a significant month.

July 1 was the first day of the month my husband was to be away for his PhD. I had assumed the significance of the month had something to do with my decision to go off birth control pills to give my body a rest for a couple of years until we officially started trying for a baby.

With this in mind, the day arrived, and I started my fast.

I was hungry, really hungry, all day at work, not feeling particularly spiritual or close to God until evening when I wandered online and searched "meaning of July 1."

The first website that came up informed me the first day of the seventh month of the lunar calendar was in fact the Jewish *Rosh HaShanah* holiday, which in the Bible is called *Yom Teruah*—the Day of Shouting, or sometimes called the Day of the Awakening Blast or the Feast of Trumpets. Even though the lunar calendar did not technically line up with July 1, I still felt drawn to read more about it. My Jewish heritage through my grandmother as well as the Jewish roots of the Christian faith were always something I had wanted to further understand.

I never randomly searched for information online, but here I was, feeling God's presence around me as I read with a sense of quiet slowness.

On the first day of the seventh month you are to have a day of sabbath rest, a sacred assembly commemorated with trumpet blasts.
—Leviticus 23:24b[2]

I learned the word *Teruah* literally means to make a loud noise, like the noise made by a *shofar* (trumpet) or by a large gathering of people shouting in unison. For example, God saying to Joshua in the Bible:

When you hear them sound a long blast on the trumpets, have the whole army give a loud shout [teruah]; then the wall of the city will collapse and the army will go up, everyone straight in.
—Joshua 6:5[3]

I got chills as I thought about my international church in Shanghai and the hundreds of us from over ninety nations on a Sunday singing and shouting out to God—the power of that cry, in unison. I loved it. I had always loved worshiping and the power of declaring truth corporately.

God, are You going to use me to rally a huge group of people to give a loud shout (teruah) at some point in my life?

I thought about one of the verses I had read on the beach when I was twelve years old.

I proclaim your saving acts in the great assembly; I do not seal my lips...

—Psalm 40:9a[4]

One of the pictures that formed in my mind that night was of me speaking in front of a great crowd of people in a huge stadium.

As I kept reading online, I learned the sounding of the trumpet on *Yom Teruah* is a wake-up blast to remind God's people that *Yom Kippur*—the Day of Atonement—is near. The ten days between *Yom Teruah* and *Yom Kippur* are considered the high holy days and are a time for examining our heart to make amends with those around us, asking for forgiveness when needed.

Not only was repentance a theme for *Yom Teruah* but also rebirth and resurrection. The trumpet blowing was a summons, a war cry, an alert warning to prepare for something, to hail an arrival or a wake-up call if one has been slumbering spiritually or physically. *Teruah* was a loud noise, a righteous noise, to stir the body, mind, and spirit to action.

At that time, I had no idea about the shaking and attack about to take place on my marriage, but what I did know deep down was I had been slumbering, waiting for Chase to move forward spiritually before I did and rushing through my life at a speed and intensity leading toward… what?

What was I so intensely doing every day? Why did I persist in allowing the Noise of condemnation and fear to drive me? The volume knob had crept up louder and louder. I was caught in it yet again, and I knew I was coping and trying to drown it out with security blankets… consuming myself with TV series, creating endless to-do lists, cramming my schedule with social appointments, getting hyper-focused on achieving my work targets, oversleeping, and leaning too much on my husband for affirmation, love, and affection.

Encounter with God had continued to feel just out of reach. Again, the perfectionistic lie had convinced me to just work a little harder to get where I needed to be, or until the next big decision. *Then* I could come to God.

I had marked July 1 in my mind as "the next big decision point" for needing God because it would be when we started to plan for a family. The date had arrived, and I knew it was now time to slow down and face all the coping I had been doing. It was time to rest and listen to God; time to get out my journal and start writing again.

So I did, and I wrote these words:

"I want to be others-focused, to be released from the prison of insecurity, doubt, and fear. Those things can really control me sometimes… often. I want my energy to be driven by the passion You have put in me."

I wanted a life not burdened by trying to control others' perceptions of me or constantly second-guessing myself. I wanted to genuinely care about others and not just spend time with them to check a box off my list.

A Bible passage I had heard recently in church really stood out to me, and I wrote it out:

And God is able to bless you abundantly, so that in all things at all times, having all that you need, you will abound in every good work… You will be enriched in every way so that you can be generous on every occasion, and through us your generosity will result in thanksgiving to God.

—*2 Corinthians 9:8, 11*[5]

That was my prayer. I wanted to learn about the spiritual realm, hear the voice of God, and receive from Him so I could be generous toward others. I wanted encounter. I wanted the stillness not just for a moment, but consistently. I wanted to be more aware of God's presence all the time.

A trumpet blast was sounding in my spirit. I knew it was time to wake up from my spiritual slumber.

CHAPTER 7

The Dead Rise

I lay awake on my side of our bed, staring blankly at the purple polka-dot curtains our landlord had picked out for our pre-furnished apartment. It was the morning after overhearing the phone call, and I listened for Chase in the house. It was quiet. He must have already left for work. I sat up slowly, crossing my arms and shivering in the Shanghai morning chill that no heater unit could ever chase out. I looked down at Chase's side of the bed—empty.

I was alone, and my insides were bursting.

What is happening? I don't understand any of this! How could Chase feel no guilt or shame? How could he act on this so quickly after just meeting her?

Then the images again—him with her, him with her, him kissing her. I couldn't breathe.

But I had to pee. I had to try to get up. That day, I had to find a counselor. I had to process this with someone and figure out what in the world was going on with my husband. I needed him desperately.

I changed into sweats and slowly pulled my mass of curly brown hair into a ponytail. Everything felt slow. Everything felt quiet. Hot tears tracked down my face as I opened my laptop and searched online for "English-speaking counselors for foreigners in Shanghai."

I dialed the first number that popped up and heard a woman's pleasant voice.

"Community Center Shanghai, how can I help you?"

"Hi, I'm... I... I need a counselor. Is anyone available today? It really needs to be today, if possible." My voice was weak.

"Hmm, well, all of our normal counselors are booked into next week, but we just had a new counselor start, and he might have an opening. One second. He is here, let me ask him... Yes, it looks like he has one slot available at eleven a.m. today. His name is Karim. Can you make it here thirty minutes early to fill out some paperwork?"

"Yes. Thank you so much. I will be there."

I stared out the glass doors of our thirteenth floor living room, gray haze hovering over dozens of apartment buildings like the haze of confusion surrounding my mind. My eyes settled on the outdoor balcony. The place Chase had been talking to... her. The warm tone in his voice... "Rachel, I love you so much." I felt sick.

What? Rachel? He lied to me. Is he talking to her right now? Thinking about her?

I squeezed my eyes shut.

This can't be real.

I shuffled slowly back to the bedroom to get my journal out of my bedside table drawer then over to the door to pull on my thick red winter coat and knock-off Ugg boots. I was moving mechanically, finding my way to the elevator, then out to the gate of my apartment compound. The Chinese security guard waved, and I managed a robotic wave back.

"*Ni hao.*"
(Hello.)

"*Ni hao.*"
(Hello.)

All seven security guards rotated, and they all knew me and Chase. We were recognizable as some of the only foreigners living in the building and always spoke to them in Chinese.

The street corner outside the gate was bustling with cars, bikes, taxis, and a street vendor selling hot steamed buns for breakfast. The familiar pink convenience store dinged its endless "someone just walked in the door" jingle next to me as I hailed a passing taxi with a "空车" (available) lighted sign at the base of the windshield. I got in, told the driver the address in Chinese, and then avoided eye contact so he wouldn't try to talk to me. No luck.

"*Ni shi faguo de ma?*"
(Are you French?)

"Bushi. Meiguo de."
(No, American.)

He broke into a huge grin and gave me a thumbs up.

"Ahhhh! Meiguo. Aobama hen hao!"
(Ahh, the US. Obama is great!)

I nodded on cue and tried to eke out a friendly smile that normally accompanied this exact carbon copy taxi conversation, but I simply couldn't. My head was still spinning, Chase's calm voice ringing in my ears. "Yes, counseling will be a good thing for you so you can start processing what I have already been processing."

How could he be so calm?

The taxi pulled up to the community center building, and I handed the driver cash. When I entered the lobby, a kind receptionist handed me a clipboard and led me to Karim's empty office to fill it out as I waited. I positioned myself on a red overstuffed chair and felt tears spilling out—dark dots appearing on the form as I ticked dozens of boxes... Not suicidal. Not depressed. Reason for visit: "Husband is in crisis. Fell in love with someone he had just met."

The door opened, and a man walked in. He was average height and appeared to be in his early forties. There was a hint of familiarity to him, like I was meeting one of my distant Middle Eastern cousins. His dark curly hair was cropped short, and his dark brown eyes were kind and safe. Their depth created immediate space to take me in. He smiled slightly, and his voice carried smooth reassurance like a hug from a longtime friend.

"Hi Corrie, I'm Karim. I recently moved to Shanghai from Canada and am glad there was an opening today for you. Let's talk about what has brought you here."

My breathing still felt staggered as I started to share. Then sobs overtook me as I tried to get it all out.

"Karim, I don't know what is happening. I've been married to Chase for six years. It's been such a good marriage, but he has been distant for months, really angry. I just found out what is really going on is that he slept with another woman, someone he had just met. I don't understand. He has experienced an extremely strong spiritual connection with this woman. I'm so confused."

Karim listened intently and compassionately as I continued to share details, pausing me initially to say, "Corrie, I want you to focus on something for a minute. You have experienced an intense trauma, and you don't need to figure it out all at once. We will talk it through, but first I need you to take a deep breath."

He inhaled deeply and then exhaled as I followed.

"Good. Now take another one."

I felt my lungs expand and then release.

"That's it. Now, take this glass of water"—he handed one to me—"and I want you to take a sip. Good. It is going to be important in these next few days and weeks to keep drinking water, keep breathing deeply. Also, you need to avoid isolating yourself. Go to work, go on walks, be active. And just keep drinking water and breathing. Can you do that?"

I nodded, sipping slowly.

"Good. Well, it certainly sounds like your husband is experiencing an existential crisis of some form. But until I meet with him, which I would like to do, I won't be able to analyze it very accurately. In the meantime, we need to focus on you."

I shifted in my chair, and he went on.

"It sounds like you have a very strong attachment to Chase. This is, of course, good, but marriages go through different phases, and normally the romantic phase is just at the beginning. What I'm hearing from you, though, is that you may still view him in a romanticized way—like an idolized version of him as part of an extended ten-year romantic phase since you first met."

I nodded again, trying to process this. He continued.

"I want you to start to focus on building your autonomy— who you are without Chase. I know you want him to choose to return to the marriage, but you need to hold that outcome loosely right now. I'm open to start meeting regularly with you and with him. I can help you start to stand on your own ground and let him discover the solution on his own."

Karim went on to share that we all have a public self, a private self, and a secret self; that maybe the secret self was something Chase had not known how to express, and that he identified with Rachel and found a sense of release. He went on to share the affair was likely a symptom of things Chase was internally wrestling with.

"Corrie, you are not to blame here. I'm not saying you're perfect, but the affair was not about you. I want to encourage you to embrace these next few weeks and months as a process. This process will be good for you. It is not a doom scenario. If you choose to embrace this process, you and Chase will both be stronger."

"Okay, Karim. Thank you so much." I let my lungs fill up then slowly release, a silent prayer flowing out with my breath.

Lord, thank You for Karim and that he was unexpectedly free today; that this affair is not about me. Help me embrace this process of building my autonomy while Chase figures things out.

I returned home and furiously journaled the entire afternoon, rarely leaving the cream-colored couch in our living room, the same place I had been sitting the night before.

Had I been living on the spiritual fumes of our early years of dating? Had I drifted with Chase spiritually in recent years? Had Chase taken more of a central role in my life than God? Had

I idolized Chase and allowed my affections to be pulled away from the Lord?

I suddenly remembered the vision our friend and groomsman, Jake, had about our marriage years before of two metals being smelted together—one representing me and one Chase—each with its own unique properties. In the heat of a huge cauldron, the impurities rose to the surface and were skimmed off as the metals forged together into one new metal with entirely new properties, not able to separate.

God, please redeem this situation with Your holy fire. Let all impurities rise to the surface.

When Chase came home, I felt drained, still desperate to try to make sense of things but also trying to be patient. He sat down on the small couch adjacent to me. I asked him questions. I couldn't help it.

"How often do you talk with her? What was happening in your mind when you decided to be with her? Were you thinking of me? Was the conversation we had on our anniversary in July real, when you told me how much you adored me, that none of the other women in your PhD program 'could hold a candle' to me'?"

He started answering the questions, the same eerie calmness over his whole countenance. The last answer shocked me. He said yes, that when he had video-Skyped with me on our sixth anniversary this past summer—tearing up and telling me how much he loved me and missed me—that he had been totally sincere with me… and that happened to be the day before he met Rachel.

"Corrie, for what it's worth, I'm really sorry you're hurting. I haven't made any big decisions yet, but I do know I can't be with her, and I've already started communicating with her less frequently. I'm still processing a lot, and I want to be open and honest with you."

Oh God, how much is too much to know?

I didn't know. Blurry confusion stung my eyes as I hugged my knees in front of me on the couch. I felt so sick to my stomach. This couldn't be real. I needed to change gears.

I managed to share with him a bit about my time with Karim, and how Karim was interested in meeting with him. To my surprise, Chase agreed to reach out to him and scheduled an appointment for the following day.

Thank You, God.

He asked if he could grab some of his clothes from our room.

"Of course," I managed.

Afterward, he passed me awkwardly en route to the guest room. Everything felt weird, off. I willed myself to stand up, then shuffled up the four stairs to our bedroom, collapsing in exhaustion.

The following day, Saturday, was a blur of more questions, more confusion. I drank more water, trying to breathe and keep moving. Every breath, every thought, every step was an effort. My physical hunger was still completely absent, vanishing along with every other sense of normalcy. I heard Chase typing and moving around in his office across the hall from the bedroom, then his hushed tone at one point as he answered a phone call.

Oh God, oh God, oh God.

Then came Sunday, the third full day of this waking nightmare. Chase was out, and this time, I couldn't get off the cream-colored couch. I lay there in terror, paralyzed and alone.

I can't lose him. He's my family. God, where are You? What are You saying? How am I supposed to go to work tomorrow? I don't know what to do. I don't know how to move forward.

Silence.

Where are You, God? What are You doing?

Silence.

Then I saw it.

A picture flashed through my mind—a circle—and on it at about eleven o'clock, a small turtle crept along counterclockwise toward the ten o'clock mark. My mind's eye studied the turtle, and a tiny laugh escaped my throat.

Chase's hilarious turtle impression was my immediate association. When he was in a silly mood, he would wrinkle up his face and neck like a turtle and eat a piece of lettuce off a fork. This image was such a comical contrast to the agony of my swirling pain. But there it was—a turtle.

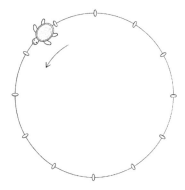

How is that my answer, Lord?

Wait, I thought. *The circle is time. It's a year.*

I knew that quite immediately as I lay there on the couch. I had always thought of a year as a circle going counterclockwise. Why? I just always had. January was at the nine o'clock mark, going into winter at eight and seven, then spring at the bottom of the circle, on around to summer on the right side at three o'clock. The turtle was positioned at the November mark, moving toward December.

Is it something with dates, God?

Yes.

I picked up my phone to look at my calendar, mouth falling open as it hit me.

Today is Sunday, November 14. That means... the day I found out about everything was... Thursday, November 11.

November 11 was *the* day. I couldn't believe it. The day everything broke; the day everything went dark; the day I felt so isolated, broken, and unseen. But I wasn't. I wasn't alone. God saw me that day. He knew that day was coming.

Oh God, thank You. You're here.

My mind kept studying the circle—a year; a turtle; *next year.* I gasped again. Next year, exactly, is... November 11, 2011.

11/11/11

I felt quiet in my spirit.

Corrie, it's going to be a year. Ride this out with me. I am redeeming your marriage. Walk that way.

I heard myself giggle, then sob. How was I laughing in this situation? I didn't know. But I could. It was right to laugh. This was it! This was my God answering me in the most personal way I could imagine.

A year of redemption culminating in elevens, my number with God... I could sense Him laughing too, in confidence— this living God of the Universe who had always seen me and known me and revealed Himself to me in little moments my whole life.

Suddenly, I knew what I needed to do.

I was to walk with God this year. I was not to walk in fear or worry or doubt about our marriage. I was to walk slowly like a turtle with full confidence in His redemption, even playful confidence.

Okay, God. I can do this. But I'm going to need a lot of "11–11 moments" this year.

Not just once a year, or every so often like it had been in my life, with so much escaping, coping, and distracting myself in between—no, now it was time to focus. I felt deep inside me this was going to be a year of discipline—discipline to stay connected to God and recenter on Him.

This would be a year of perpetual fasting. Fasting from my husband as well as from so many other things that had suddenly melted out of my life—the need to please others, be superficial in any way, watch TV, stuff myself with food, fill my schedule… *gone*, suddenly.

I shifted to a seated position on the couch and opened up my Bible. The words soaked in.

As the deer pants for streams of water, so my soul pants for you, my God. My soul thirsts for God, for the living God. When can I go and meet with God? My tears have been my food day and night…

Why, my soul, are you downcast? Why so disturbed within me?
Put your hope in God, for I will yet praise Him, my Savior and
my God.

—*Psalm 42:1–3a, 5*[1]

I sat in the quiet of my apartment and reflected, prayed, and journaled. Raw, refreshing honesty rushed out of me onto the pages, and a beautiful stillness interrupted the chaos of the previous days and months.

This was the beginning of my journey with God through pain—a picture of a turtle walking around the circle of a year. A simple image to remind me how to walk burned onto my consciousness.

It was no guarantee that Chase would return to reconcile with me—though I was convinced he would. Rather, it was an invitation for me to walk in the way of truth—the truth of God's heart for our marriage. The alternative? Operating from a fearful place of Chase not returning and living from that place had crushed me the previous few days.

I needed to remain in the posture of hope and keep my feet on the circle with my hand in God's hand, like balancing on a tiny tightrope of light over a black vortex of fear, destruction, insecurity, mocking accusation, confusion, and hopelessness—so godless and menacing and black.

I needed to remember I wasn't alone.

The couch creaked as I rose up.

CHAPTER 8

Time to Be Fierce

The lush green grass of the mountain top had an ethereal glow and formed a soft carpet to cushion us as we reclined on our picnic blanket. We drank in the sun-soaked beauty of nature around us as we ate and chatted leisurely. It was me, Chase, and a new couple we were just getting to know.

Chase's eyes were relaxed and kind. I was in the middle of a long explanation about something to the couple, but it was clear from the wife's face she was not understanding me. Without hesitation, Chase jumped in.

"No, no, no, this is Corrie just externally processing. It's what she does."

Warmth for my husband flooded my senses. I loved being known so fully that even my personality quirks, like never being able to tell a brief story, were considered endearing.

After the picnic, we found ourselves strolling down a path to the couple's gorgeous wooden chalet-style house, situated on the side of the mountain. Once inside the kitchen, the wife smiled and handed me a small note, tightly folded up. Intrigued, I started unfolding its many sections. It was like a map, filled with tiny green writing—encouraging words just for me. I stood there stunned and touched by this unexpected gesture from a near stranger.

I could only scan the note, though, because at that moment, the house and land shook and cracked as if an earthquake and an avalanche had hit us simultaneously. The whole world shifted in an instant, and the four of us were suddenly back outside being swept away in a huge round floating raft. We watched in shock as the mountains crumbled around us into a boiling and swirling sea.

Clinging to the raft in the turbulent water, we gasped in horror as a black cloud rose in front of us up the gray sky, slowly taking shape into a massive demonic woman. My hair whipped violently around my face and my trembling shoulders as two evil daggers of yellow glared down at us from the raging black cloud. She dwarfed our tiny raft and mocked us with a voice like thunder, hurling down taunts and accusations as lightning cracked and flashed around her.

Terrified, the four of us cowered face down in the raft, hands over our heads.

Then I felt it. A stirring deep inside of me, an energy rising up from a new yet strangely familiar place—righteous anger paired with deep compassion. It came to me quickly, and then I knew, as if I'd always known.

This is who I really am. This is what I was made for.

My eyes narrowed and set as I stood up slowly to turn and face the giant terror, the huge storm of a woman. Raising my fist in the air, my voice rang out boldly above the crash of the waves.

"Jesus is Lord! Jesus is Lord! Jesus is Lord!"

Poof! Calm—a complete scene change. I found myself in a serene and peaceful park. The terrifying woman had become a tiny speck, a dandelion puff floating on the breeze in the sunlight. I followed her intently with my eyes, switching from my battle cry to a whisper.

"Jesus is Lord. You can know Him. It's simple. You can accept Him as Lord of your life."

The strange boldness grew stronger in me, like I knew the outcome. The dandelion puff disappeared, becoming at once a lovely young woman—average size and frame. She sat there calmly on the path, looking at me with sincerity and relief.

"I believe," she said.

My eyes darted open as the golden morning shone through the purple polka-dot curtains. My pulse was a drumbeat in my ears as I lied there, stunned at the clarity of this dream and also perplexed about its meaning.

Who was the first woman, God, and what did her green-lettered note say? Who was the demon woman?

Chase had been sleeping in the guest room for almost two weeks now, and I desperately missed our closeness. His affirming words to me at the picnic felt like a warm sweater I got to wear all day as I pondered the dream, even while biking back home after work in the biting wind of Shanghai. Strangely, it didn't feel as cold as it normally did in November.

While alone in the apartment while Chase was still out at a work dinner, I journaled for over an hour. This had become my daily ritual. I thought back to each scene of the dream, coming back again and again to what felt even more significant than the kind words from my husband.

It was the stirring I had felt when I was cowering in the raft—that sense I was created to stand up and fight.

How did I know what to do?

I just did. I had never felt so bold, so fierce.

A part of me had been cowering for a long time. I could feel it, and I knew it deep down. Fear and accusations had been on stereo in my mind since childhood, sometimes blaring and sometimes like a low buzz of white noise.

Since overhearing the November 11 phone call, lies had been tormenting me—lies I wasn't good enough, smart enough, attractive enough, intellectual enough, or opinionated enough to keep my husband from doing what he did… that I wasn't enough.

I knew it was time to stop cowering. Now, it was time to be fierce.

CHAPTER 9

Broken Lives Meet

It's a strange thing to not be hungry, to have no desire for food at all, I thought as I scootered to church, having no clue about the challenge from God that awaited me there.

I had eaten almost nothing in the three weeks since November 11, and there was an odd relief in it, like a fog in front of me had suddenly cleared. What was this quietness? Somehow, I knew I needed it.

Then would come the waves of tormenting confusion swirling and pounding against my head.

Oh God, oh God, oh God. How could this be? How could this be?

Every moment in those days was a prayer—crying out, listening, crying out, listening—as I walked in the hope of His redemption for my marriage. Every moment was a conscious step to stay on the circle with God—the tightrope of light over the menacing black vortex.

My scooter brakes screeched as I pulled up onto the curb and fastened my lock around a lamp post on Heng Shan Road, across the street from our church. The towering red-brick

A-frame building was covered in large panels of stained glass and stood prominently in the French district of Shanghai. This neighborhood's avenues were lined with trees and stately century-old houses, as well as popular bars and restaurants. It always felt peaceful at this time of day, before the nightclubs started hopping.

I checked my watch—three minutes to 4:00 p.m., the best time ever for church if you're a night owl like me.

Being surrounded by people from over ninety nations each week at Shanghai Community Fellowship's international service was always refreshing. Our congregation was permitted to use the beautiful arced sanctuary only at this time because several Chinese services, kept separate and run by the government-supervised church, happened there in the morning. We, as foreigners, could attend the Chinese services, but Chinese nationals were not permitted to attend ours. No one at church knew the details of my situation yet.

As I ran across the street with my purse and Bible, I spied the familiar huddle of Chinese beggars who hovered around the gate between services. The sun glinted off the wheelchair of a severely crippled man, Duyi, who I'd been seeing there recently and briefly chatting with in my limited Chinese. His mom was a small yet determined woman by her son's chair. Her tired eyes still carried a sparkle.

"*KeKe!*"
(Corrie!)

Their voices carried a bit of urgency as they gestured for me to come over. I fidgeted with my purse in a moment of slight hesitation then walked over to respond.

Duyi's navy pants were dusty and knotted conspicuously just below his knees, extra fabric dangling above empty footrests. His gnarled fists were covered with white callouses, and he beamed up at me with noticeably straight white teeth. A black beanie covered his bald head down to the place his eyebrows should have been, and small patches of peeling white skin interrupted the smooth redness of his cheeks.

He held something out with scabbed stubs, once his fingers.

"*Zhege shi wo ziji zuode, yao songgei ni.*"
(This is something I made myself. It's a gift for you.)

It was a tiny plastic ziplock bag with what looked like a colorful mini set of origami cranes pressed together inside. What a surprise. I was touched but was also feeling a flush of awkwardness in this setting. I had said hello to Duyi the past few weeks but had never given him any money. Leaders at church always recommended giving food instead.

"*Duyi, ni hen bang! Xiexie ni a.*"
(Duyi, you are wonderful. Thank you so much.)

I smiled and waved as I turned to slip through the church gate, backing awkwardly away from the hopeful hands of several others reaching my way.

The musty air of the aged building smelled familiar and homey to me now after four years in Shanghai, and I quickly took my normal seat in the front-right section of the huge sanctuary just as the opening song came to a close. The long bench pews were dark glossy wood, quite a bit harder than the padded version in my childhood church in Northern Virginia.

As the welcome and announcements began, I pulled the tiny ziplock from my pocket. The four tiny paper cranes were connected with string, perfectly spaced apart as a single-strand mobile. I let it drop and dangle in front of me.

How did he manage this with such limited dexterity in his partial fingers?

Take him to dinner.

The thought popped into my consciousness and would not leave.

Take him to dinner.

God, is that You? No way. That's crazy! No!

Ask him. Tonight.

God, I can't. That is too weird.

Trust me. Take him to dinner.

But I don't want to. That's weird. I'm not ready. Maybe next time.

I turned my attention to the worship music and then the sermon, trying to forget the idea. Our American pastor was reading out a section from the Bible, but I struggled to focus.

Take him to dinner.

I twiddled the origami cranes through my anxious fingers and remembered the warmth that had filled me just an hour earlier when Duyi had proudly held up his homemade gift. And now I was grimacing, wincing in discomfort.

I don't want to get involved, God. I know this would not just be one step. It would be the first of many. Ahh… It's just too complicated. Too uncertain. I hate this feeling!

Corrie, I'm in this. Trust me.

But God, I'm hurting too much. I can't give anything right now. My marriage just broke. I'm hurting so badly.

I know. I have a plan. Just take him to dinner.

I wrestled back and forth, finding any and all reasons to resist. But I was desperate inside to stay close to God. I was desperate to follow Him around the circle and not miss anything He might be doing along the way to bring my husband back. I truly sensed this instruction was from God, and I couldn't ignore it.

Argh! Okay, God. Okay.

I built up my resolve as I waited for the closing cadences of the worship music, willed myself to get up, and then almost robotically marched out to the church gates. Duyi and his mom were there, and I motioned for them to move to the side, away from earshot of the others. I contemplated just giving them the 50 RMB bill in my pocket (roughly $7), but instead, I forced out the words I had mentally rehearsed in the pews as sincerely as I could muster.

"Nimen yao gen wo yiqi qu chifan ma? Wo yao qing nimen."
(Would you two like to come with me to dinner? I would like to treat you.)

"Zai fandian ma?"
(At a restaurant?)

"Dui. Fujin youde."
(Yes. There is one close by.)

"Dangran! Women yiqi qu ba."
(Of course! We'll go with you.)

Their eyes twinkled as they turned to follow me up the street, mother pushing son rather quickly as to not draw further attention. I knew of a medium-sized Sichuan-style restaurant around the corner and tried to walk confidently.

My mind seized.

Would they even have wheelchair access?

They did. I blew out my breath, heart beating through my chest as I ignored the puzzled look on the hostess's face when she saw my guests. I stumbled over my words as I asked her where the nearest available table was on the ground floor. She walked us over, trying to follow my very imperfect Chinese instructions to move two of the chairs to the corner of the room to make room for his... uh... chair? I didn't know the word for wheelchair.

She and the server shuffled the chairs around and created a space for Duyi to be wheeled in. And then we sat. I ordered a few standard dishes, and they just smiled back at me, insisting I not get anything too expensive.

Okay, God. Here I am.

The conversation started. They were from the countryside, central China. "Where?" I asked as my thoughts wandered to the one place I knew in central China—Jingzhou, a small city. Chase and I had visited years ago to see friends who were teaching English out in the middle of nowhere.

They smiled and said I probably wouldn't know the place. It was outside of Wuhan, a city named Jingzhou.

"Jingzhou?" I almost dropped my hand sanitizer.

They answered yes, and I told them about my connection to the city and that I had been there. They were amazed—immediate common ground.

The food arrived, and I was surprised to feel a few hints of hunger. I asked if I could pray. They said yes and that they were followers of *Yesu* (Jesus).

"I am too!" I exclaimed.

I sat there further stunned, then bowed my head, nervously trying to think of which Chinese words would fit best together for a prayer over the food. Before I had voiced anything, though, I heard whispers and peeked to notice Duyi and his mom were already talking to God. Both of them were whispering phrases with heads bowed, pouring out their hearts. I sat there in awe with no words except *God, help* coming to mind as I faced the impossible situation in front of me.

This thirty-five-year-old man had suffered from a rare skin condition since he was three years old. The condition had literally eaten away his feet, lower legs, and hands while also causing rough skin to grow out of control even on his head and face. These areas had to be scrubbed daily to keep his skin clear.

And there he sat, joy and life coming out of him as he carefully lifted food to his mouth with chopsticks.

"What are you doing here in Shanghai?" he asked.

I chose my words carefully, trying to decide if I would just talk about myself or my husband as well.

I told them I worked in a bilingual school with students from two to eighteen years old and that my team's job was to help the foreign parent visitors decide if it was the right school for their children.

"No wonder you speak Chinese so well!" they remarked.

And then the dreaded question.

"Where is your husband?"

I sighed, unsure how to respond yet feeling strangely comfortable.

"He… He is in Shanghai, but he… is having some difficulty, some big anxieties," I managed.

Two sets of compassionate eyes stared back at me, taking in what I said.

"We will definitely pray for him."

A hot tear trickled down my cheek as Duyi went on.

"*Keke* (Corrie), I must tell you. Since my mom and I became believers two years ago, we have felt an overwhelming feeling of peace in our lives. All of our *fannao* (worries) used to weigh on us so heavily, but after praying and knowing *Yesu* (Jesus), He lifted them off of us."

I felt activated, engrossed. This conversation was not hard anymore.

You set me up, God. You knew I would be okay.

His mom went on with their story.

"We still struggle every day though. We came to Shanghai from Jingzhou to get Duyi's medicine that was prescribed here. It is so hard to afford it, and so he is now taking just half a pill per day instead of the full pill."

She paused and looked with concern at her son.

"So his joints are getting stiffer, and the skin layers tougher. Thanks to God and His grace, I still am able to help Duyi, and a very close sister in Christ from the church was able to help pay for and arrange his leg amputation surgery last year. It was such a blessing."

As she finished, an idea sprouted up in my mind. *I wonder if maybe some friends and I in my small group could help them with the medicine issue?*

"*Duyi de yao shi duoshao qian?*" I asked his mom.
(How much is Duyi's medicine?)

"*Meitian 50 renminbi,*" they responded.
(About 50 RMB [$7] per day.)

I smiled.

"I will pray about it and ask my friends from church. We might be able to help contribute to help him get his full pill every day," I told them.

"*Ganxie Zhu! Ganxie Zhu,*" they exclaimed.
(Thank You, God! Thank You, God!)

As his mom wheeled him out of the restaurant that brisk fall evening, a piece of heaviness lifted off of me. My heart was filled and moved.

God, You love these people. And we can actually connect.

My pain, brokenness, and desperation for God had slowed me down and opened time and space to connect with these two people who God loved. Although my own pain could not remotely compare to the extreme desperation Duyi and his mom experienced daily, I was somehow being activated to notice and connect more with them and with others in pain.

Thank You, God, for being here. You see me. You see Duyi and his mom. You're doing something. Somehow, it's all connected. I can't see the full picture yet, but I would have never reached out to them if I hadn't been in my crisis.

I've never been this desperate, God. I've never needed You so much. I've never been this quiet to listen. But I'm hearing now. I'm listening. I'm following. Thank You for quieting the Noise.

Heal Duyi's broken body, and heal my broken heart.

My small group indeed agreed to help Duyi, and we formed a significant and lasting friendship with him over the next months and years, even to this very day.

CHAPTER 10

Out of the Shadows

"I can't hold it in anymore."

On a Sunday evening after church in mid-January of 2011, I sat with legs crossed on Leanna's blue-striped couch, trying to control my breathing. My pulse was racing in time with my shaking foot.

This couch, like my cream-colored one, had been a place of many tears the previous few months. I had been coming here each Thursday night for small group Bible study.

The group was mostly comprised of young, expatriate ("expat") couples and a few singles who lived in nearby neighborhoods and attended Shanghai Community Fellowship international church. Our times of group Bible study were often followed by splitting up into guys' and girls' groups for more sharing and prayer.

Leanna and James had been the first couple in the group to announce a pregnancy. At this stage, Leanna's belly extended prominently and affectionately toward me as she leaned in to grab my hands, her large blue eyes blinking in concern.

"What is it?" Her Canadian accent was subtle compared to the very distinctive and melodious British accent of her husband, James, who was perched beside her with the same intent look.

Interestingly, it had been Chase who had originally heard about this group through some new guy friends at church, just a few months before the disastrous happenings of July 2010. It had been Chase who initiated inviting Leanna and James over for dinner at our place around that same time, excited to be making a group of new friends since many of ours had moved away from Shanghai in 2009.

I had shared Chase's enthusiasm about this new group, and from our first time attending, we immediately felt at home with these new friends from Australia, Canada, the UK, the US, Singapore, Malaysia, New Zealand, and Germany.

"These are our people! Like instant family," I remember telling Chase after we attended the small group for the first time.

He nodded. "What an answer to prayer."

As expats, we were all living away from our families and all familiarity, trying our best with the Chinese language, and having daily adventures in Shanghai as we navigated either language studies or a range of jobs in education or business.

Up to this point, all Leanna and James knew was what I had been telling them since last summer—that Chase was struggling with some kind of inner turmoil and needed prayer. From November 11 forward, I had been carefully crafting my message to leave out the revelation of the affair and Chase moving out. I had been in such a state of shock and codependence that I had let Chase control the situation. He had not wanted me to share the details with people, so I hadn't. I had been terrified he would get upset with me and divorce me to go to *her*, the unthinkable scenario.

But that time was over. My foot was still shaking.

"It… It's Chase. After small group one night in November, I overheard a phone call. He's in love with someone else. He met her last summer…"

My hands trembled as the story tumbled out—how I had been trying to explore an uninterrupted dialogue process with just Chase and the counselor to first try and understand what in the world was going on with him, that the private process had lasted two months and had been helpful in many ways, but the previous week, I had found out Chase's affair had resumed during his trip to the US, even though he insisted it was over, and that I had lost my will to keep covering for him.

The privacy was no longer fruitful and was leading to more confusion, destruction, and pain, not to mention the fact I had already lost twenty pounds. I needed more support. I had finally broken down and told my parents a few days before, and Leanna and James were the first friends I was sharing it with.

Leanna's eyes were wide, her palm covering her mouth.

"Bloody hell!" James shook his head and slammed his fist into his hand. "What was the silly bugger thinking?"

James's anger and protective older brother energy hit me like a refreshing splash of cold water, a little jolt of freedom to access the emotion of anger for the very first time. I sank back against the blue-striped cushion, exhaling deeply.

"So, you've been living on your own since early December? *He moved out?*" Leanna asked.

I nodded, tears spilling down my cheeks as I slowly started rocking back and forth. What a relief to be sharing freely.

"Who else knows?" James asked.

"Just my counselor Karim, and my parents and siblings so far. I'm planning to tell the rest of the small group and the pastor's wife in the next few days. I'm then planning to confront Chase next Saturday during Chinese New Year to let him know I've told my family and close friends and that I'm not willing to keep his secret anymore."

I paused, weighing my words.

"I'm going to give him two weeks to share with his family, boss, and close friends, if he wants them to hear it from him first. He's not going to be happy, and I'm terrified, but I've prayed about it. I think it's something I need to do if we are going to have an authentic process moving forward."

They asked a few more questions then proceeded to douse me with encouragement.

"You know you are absolutely amazing. Clearly this is not about you, Corrie. It is not your fault. We are here for you every step of the way."

I beamed at them, face still wet and shining. "Thank you."

I will never forget what happened next. They gave each other a quick knowing glance and then Leanna turned to look me dead in the eyes. Her tone was loving and resolute.

"Corrie, dinner here is at six p.m. You are part of our family now, and we will expect you here every night at that time unless you tell us otherwise. Understood?"

I nodded as I got up to leave, eyes blurry with tears. They both hugged me fiercely.

I clutched my jacket close as I made the brisk five-minute walk back to my apartment complex, which happened to be on the same street, literally adjacent to theirs. My heart felt alive and warm.

Oh Lord, how is it that You arranged, through Chase no less, to bring a whole new group of friends into my life just in time? Friends who know and love both me and Chase. Friends who know You. Friends who are like family. What a gift!

I got a phone call the next day from my little brother, Tim, who had been the original China pioneer among my siblings.

He had been living and working for five years already in Beijing.

"Corrie, I'm flying down to be with you next week during Chinese New Year. I'll be there the day before the confrontation. You can't be alone for this."

It was a moment in time. Support started coming out of the woodwork, and I started to eat again, slowly but surely.

The daily dinners started at Leanna's that evening, and James was an absolute master in the kitchen. I feasted both on homemade meals and undivided loving attention from them, a safe place for my tears and endless processing. Sometimes conversations went deep, and other times they were light, a welcome relief from the heaviness of my pain.

My close girl friends from small group came around me with fierce support and planned a prayer night at my apartment for the following Tuesday, February 1. It was the night before the biggest holiday week in China—start of the lunar new year. I ordered chicken pesto pasta for everyone from Wagas, a popular western café, and passed around individual containers of it as the ladies filed in.

"Thanks so much for coming, ladies. We really need to pray for Chase right now. He is in such a rough place," I started.

My friend Ava chimed in immediately. "Yes, for sure. But, Corrie, what about you? How are *you* doing?" Ten pairs of eyes looked back at me with love and concern.

I blinked. "I'm okay. I mean, I'm hurting, of course, but Chase is the one who is really hurting."

"Corrie," Ava continued, "we are definitely praying for Chase, but I also want to really encourage you to think about you. What do you need?" The others nodded.

"You guys, I so appreciate that, and one of my major needs was to share with you, which has been so helpful. But this whole thing is not about me. I'm not the one going through a faith and identity crisis. It's Chase!"

I struggled to understand their insistence. In my mind, nothing was more central than Chase coming back and getting the support he needed.

"Corrie, this is about you too. You're going through something catastrophic. You've been severely betrayed. You've been holding all of this in for more than two months. You're thin as a rail. And you need time and space to heal. We are here for you, and you need to know that your needs are very important too."

Something clicked in me when she said that. Chase had been absolutely first in my mind, first in my thoughts daily, first in my prayers. I remembered Karim's words: "Corrie, I want you to start to focus on building your autonomy."

I had started taking small steps, but maybe I needed more. Maybe this crisis wasn't just about sorting out Chase's issues and praying he would return. Maybe I had some work to do—to learn how to receive love and how not to prioritize Chase's needs over my own.

The question "Corrie, what do *you* need?" stuck with me as the ladies shuffled out and as I packed my bag for a three-day solo trip to the mountains.

I thought about it on the two-hour train ride out of Shanghai to the scenic lake city of Hangzhou and then on the six-hour bus ride up to a guest house a friend had recommended. A place with snow falling off branches into the stillness of fresh, clean mountain air. A place where the rural family who owned the guest house invited me to eat with them and cooked dozens of fresh dishes from their garden. A place where Chinese New Year fireworks blasted into the evening as the teenaged son taught me how to play *majiang* (mahjong) in Chinese. A place where roosters woke me up the next two mornings. A place where I gathered my courage and made my plan to confront Chase.

So many people were praying for me and starting to send me daily encouragement. An email from my mom was on my mind as I ran through potential reactions from Chase.

> Corrie, you asked us to relay to you any pictures or thoughts we received during this week. As I was praying for you yesterday, a picture came to mind of a caught fish lying on the dock in its last stages before death, mouth occasionally opening and closing. It was very, very clear, no sound, just opening and closing of its mouth. That's all. I am praying this is Chase's heart, ready to die to the confusion in its last stages this week

before repentance and death to self. Oh, God, I pray this is so. I love you, Corrie.

Mom

I played out scenario after scenario in my mind. When the bus arrived back in Hangzhou, I walked by the lake while I waited for my train, talking with my dad, who had called me to role-play the encounter, on the phone. I was ready, as ready as I could be.

I arrived back in Shanghai Friday evening, refreshed and also terrified about Saturday. My brother had already arrived from Beijing and had let himself into my apartment with the key I had left for him. He hugged me tightly as I walked in the door.

"You got this."

The next morning, I awoke to the smell of buttered toast.

CHAPTER 11

A Breakthrough and a New Routine

"Almost ready!" Tim yelled from the kitchen.

"You shopped?" I asked.

"Yep," he said. "You needed some food around here."

He came out with two plates of scrambled eggs and toast. I noticed the jam was spread on haphazardly as he poured me a glass of apple juice.

"You need to eat."

I sipped slowly on the apple juice… delicious. I had never bought apple juice in Shanghai.

What a strange thing—to have someone serve me.

I got up to help.

"Nope. I got it." He smiled. "You just eat, and I'll clean up after. Then I'll make myself scarce and go walk around in the city, so when Chase comes, you can have your talk."

I took another sip of the apple juice, drinking in this small but powerful act of love from my brother. My little brother, taking care of me. I liked this. Someone thinking about me, taking care of me. Still strange, but I liked it. Could I dare to say I need this?

Lord, I pray for protection for me and for Chase. For confidence and conviction for me to speak and declare the truth in love, a truth that will pierce, that will shed light through the fog and darkness surrounding him.

The afternoon came, and Chase arrived. He looked tired as he walked in and sat across from me on the accent chair.

I mustered up all my courage and told him my family and close friends were now in the loop and that it was helping me. That I needed support. That I had trusted him to stay committed to the process of counseling and figuring things out together, but that trust had been broken again by his continued affair. That he had two weeks to share with his boss and his friends. That his boss needed to be in the loop since Chase was in a position of Christian leadership and mentorship to his students in the program.

"You told them without discussing it with me?" Chase threw his hands in the air and stared me down. "This is crossing a line, Corrie. I have been trying very hard to try to figure things out with you in the context of counseling. This is just too much. I can't believe you did this."

I had prepared for this response and focused on steadying my breath.

"Chase, I really need this, and I think it will be good for both of us. We need to bring people in. We need their support and perspective."

He got up and walked to the door, steps firm and pounding. He grabbed his coat and grasped the door handle.

"Corrie, I tried. I really tried. And then you just go off and ruin our chances for reconciliation. Take care of yourself."

I jumped as the door slammed, fingers trembling as I picked up my phone and dialed Tim's number.

"He's gone. You can come back now."

I stayed up most of the night praying, shaken and quiet.

Oh God, please give Chase wisdom to distinguish lies from the truth. Will You please lead him to repentance and godly sorrow over what he has done? Help him recognize he needs to get things into the light and receive help, that he does not have all the answers.

My phone buzzed the next morning. It was a text from Chase. "Can I come over?"

My thumb trembled as I sent the text reply. "Okay."

I threw on sweats, splashed water on my face, and woke my brother up to ask him to head out again so Chase and I could talk privately.

"I think he's coming to tell me he's going to divorce me," I said.

Tim was calm and resolute. "Whatever it is, you did the right thing, Corrie. If he does say that, he will be the biggest idiot on the planet. Just text me when you want me to come back."

Just a few minutes after Tim left, I heard a soft knock. I took a deep breath, walked over, and turned the handle. I spied the dark circles under Chase's eyes at first but then was drawn up to his gaze. Instead of the faraway look I had seen there, I noticed a different intensity, more alertness.

"Hi."

"Hi." I looked down, heart pounding in my chest.

He stepped inside and stammered, "I was up all night. I couldn't sleep and was praying, and…" He reached out to touch my shoulder.

I wrinkled my brow.

"I'm just… I really…" He sputtered as he leaned against me. I put an arm around him and then staggered back under his weight.

"Corrie, I'm sorry…. I'm so, so sorry."

His shoulders started to shake uncontrollably, and I tried to process what was happening. All I knew was that he was not going to be able to keep standing. I stepped backward and moved him over toward the couch. As I sat down, he dropped to his knees, head down as sobs poured out of him.

"What I did… It was wrong. It was wrong. I see that now. I'm so, so sorry. It was wrong." Tears and snot gushed out of him like a faucet as I cradled his head in my lap.

My husband. There you are.

I was too in shock, too relieved, and too intrigued to cry. I felt a sudden expansion in my chest, like I was taking my first breath in months. Like I had been underwater for minutes and was breaking through the surface.

Oh my gosh. God, You're doing it.

Bleary blue eyes peered up at me, and I brushed his hair back.

"I forgive you, Chase. I forgive you. I love you so much." The words flowed out like water. His sobs were quieter now.

How I've missed you, love. Where have you been?

His breaths were heavy as he rested his head on my lap. There was no "I love you" back. I waited, wondering—nothing.

After what seemed like thirty minutes but was probably only nine or ten, I got up to get him a tissue, and we sat together on the cream-colored couch. His words were shaky but decisive as he told me he planned to call his boss to talk to him, as well as his family and close friends. We briefly talked about the counseling session we had coming up the following week, after the holiday ended.

There was not much more to say after that, it seemed. We were both exhausted, and I was still in a bit of shock. Chase broke the silence.

"Do you mind if I get a few things on my way out?"

"Of course. That's fine."

He padded up our four stairs to grab some clothes and papers from his office, then came to give me a hug on his way out. I held onto him for a few deep breaths and then watched him walk out. No kiss. Still no "I love you."

But my heart felt strangely light.

Thank You, Lord. Thank You, thank You, thank You. This was a direct answer to prayer. You're helping him see truth. Thank You.

Tim came back a few minutes later. It turns out he had run into Chase on his way out in the hallway and had given him a hug.

"Chase looked beat," he said.

I smiled slowly and shared about the blurry, bizarre encounter. Dark spots remained on my jeans, no longer large splotches.

Did that really just happen?

I sat down to journal and realized something fundamental had shifted in me on the days leading up to the confrontation. I was no longer on Chase's team. I couldn't be. I couldn't be his "figure it out together" person anymore. I wasn't his mother or his mentor. I was his wife, and I needed to heal. I needed to be around people who loved me and massively limit my exposure to Chase. That became crystal clear. I was now on the team of the people who loved me, and I was to lean onto them for wisdom while I got my cues from God, no longer from Chase. I didn't need to analyze everything or focus all my energy on Chase's process anymore.

God, look what You did! Help me to keep trusting You. You are the only one who can help Chase sort through the mess he is in.

Chase had always been so self-assured, so "right" about things. He had always been so respected, so put together, such a solid Christian leader. Finally, the fog had cleared. I had idolized him. His view of things had been my view of things. His opinions of things were central to me. He was central to me.

And now he was off the pedestal. Now he was "out *there*," and I was holding the hand of God "right *here*." I drew a big hand in my journal as I sensed this new picture—my tiny little hand in the biggest hand in the universe. God was trustworthy. When I had trusted His view of things and not Chase's, Chase had experienced a breakthrough.

I took another huge breath in. Many more breakthroughs were needed, but what a first step.

I started walking this new path just as new baby Charla made her perfectly timed appearance into the world. My new dinner routine at Leanna and James's house became more life-giving than ever.

Charla was the type of baby who could only sleep "on" someone in the baby carrier for a while, so when I could, I "wore" her for a few hours to give them a break, sometimes until the wee hours of the morning, walking and bouncing and feeling the comfort of this little sleeping life against me. My tears would drip down onto her little fuzzy blonde head, and she would just coo and snore and receive the love I had to give. I was receiving it too.

Being around her and having this new dinner routine was so healing. With this in mind, one day, I thought about my previous lunch break routine at work, which was to give Chase a quick call just to say hi, check in with him, and say I love you. I missed that every day and felt a stinging hole in its place.

"Leanna, could I call you on my lunch break just to say hi and chat about the day a bit?" I asked at small group, taking a leap.

"Sure, I would love that!" she said.

For months, I called for those few minutes each day. The relief of talking to someone who *wanted* to talk to me gave me something small to look forward to in my pain-filled life.

I found little ways to thank Leanna besides baby time. I recognized my spoken Chinese was at a place I could communicate more complicated ideas than she could to the locals, and I was thinking one day about her new curtains sitting in a pile on her floor. For months, she had been meaning to get them shortened to fit her windows.

The idea was simple, but the thought of it gave me this little surge of joy. I called her and offered to take them to a Chinese tailor I knew at the local market. She was ecstatic, and I realized the extra time I had while Chase was "away" was not always best spent on my own, where I would be tempted to spiral downward.

Spending alone time journaling and thinking was critical for me in those early months of 2011, but a few times a week, it gave me life to fill some of my extra time helping my friends.

For those who had small children, I became "Auntie Coco" and kicked them out to go for a date night while I played for hours with their kids. I had never really liked playing with kids before then. I was good at doing the responsible stuff like feeding them, bathing them, and getting them to bed, but the imaginative play part had never been appealing to me. This changed during the pain years.

I loved being with kids. Sometimes I only wanted to be with kids. They just "got it" and were the best huggers, and when I was in pain, being around them was so healing. There was no pretense with kids. Just love and presentness and play— the way I felt as I grasped the giant hand of the God of the Universe. Playful, present, and full of hope.

This was the God who had set me up, just months before the affair, to meet new friends who lived five minutes away from me. This was the God who provided new routines and a baby to cuddle with, the God who provided a brother to fly down and pour me apple juice before the hardest conversation of my life, and the God who was working on the heart of my husband as part of His redemption plan.

God, I'm so sorry I've allowed Chase to be central in my life. I want You to be central. Things will only work if You are central.

CHAPTER 12

The Prayer Warrior

For where two or three gather in my name, there am I with them.
—Matthew 18:20

On a Friday night at 6:30 p.m., about a month after I started being open with my close friends about my marriage crisis and separation, I sat at a small table for two at the Wagas Café down the street from my apartment.

I had no idea what to expect.

All I knew was a woman from church I had never met, Jody, had offered to come meet me. She was a close friend of my pastor's wife, Bella, who had shared with her about my situation. Bella had texted me saying simply that Jody wanted to meet me in person. I was open to anything so had agreed to connect with her.

A petite middle-aged woman burst through the glass door, made eye contact, and walked straight over to me.

"*Corrie*! Hi, I'm Jody."

She gave me a firm handshake then an immediate hug, her pale blue eyes smiling and alive with intensity.

Her voice had a lower register than I was expecting and a bit of a raspy quality, like she had just been cheering and yelling at a basketball game for the last few hours. An American who had lived in China for over a decade, she was no frills and no-nonsense, dressed in a casual pink hoodie and sweat pants and ready for action. A white scrunchy held her ashy blonde hair back into a short, youthful ponytail.

Jody took an intentional seat across from me at the table and grabbed both of my hands. I was a bit taken aback by her directness and lack of any small talk, but I quickly adjusted as I recognized a spiritual giant was before me. Her words were steady, confident, and sure.

"Now, tell me… What do you know about spiritual warfare?"

I blinked, stammering.

"Um…. Well, honestly, not a ton. I do know about the armor of God in Ephesians 6, where it says our struggle is not against flesh and blood but instead against spiritual forces of evil in the heavenly realms."

"*Yes!* That is a great place to start." Jody smiled and pumped her fist in the air. "There is a spiritual war going on—forces of evil that want to take you down, take down your marriage, and take down your husband."

She opened her Bible and started reading with strength and conviction. She slid her finger under each word as she read, drawing me in to follow.

Humble yourselves, therefore, under God's mighty hand, that he may lift you up in due time. Cast all your anxiety on him because he cares for you. Be alert and of sober mind.

our enemy the devil prowls around like a roaring lion looking for someone to devour. Resist him, standing firm in the faith... and the God of all grace, who called you to his eternal glory in Christ, after you have suffered a little while, will himself restore you and make you strong, firm, and steadfast.

—1 Peter 5:6–9a, 10¹

Jody paused and looked up.

"We are mighty warriors, and we have to be on the offensive against the enemy. The enemy will not push us around. We will push the enemy around."

She flipped through some pages and continued reading.

For though we live in the world, we do not wage war as the world does. The weapons we fight with are not the weapons of the world.

On the contrary, they have divine power to demolish strongholds. We demolish arguments and every pretension that sets itself up against the knowledge of God, and we take captive every thought to make it obedient to Christ.

—2 Corinthians 10:3-5[2]

She tapped her finger on the page.

"There are two realities—the physical reality and the spiritual reality. I have learned not to base what I think and do on the physical reality but instead to walk and fight according to the Spirit, looking at the *spiritual* reality. The moment I heard about your story from Bella, I knew in my *spirit*"—she pointed to her heart—"I was to pray with you and teach you how to pray, if you're open to that."

Something stirred deep within me, and I realized I was slowly nodding.

"Yes, of course. I'm very open to that." My words sounded so hesitant and flighty compared to hers.

She went on with continued intensity.

"I only operate by assignment from the Holy Spirit, and this is the assignment He has put on my heart. I don't take His assignments lightly. Let me tell you about my last one."

She told me the story of standing and warring in prayer with her Chinese neighbor, Maya, who was a new believer in Jesus. Maya's husband, Clark, had abandoned her and their son for another woman and new life. After almost a year of praying,

Clark came to faith and fully surrendered his life to God. He returned to the family and completely reconciled with Maya.

Jody paused, and then she asked me about my situation with Chase. Tears streamed down my face as I shared the latest.

"I think he's still in love with this woman he knew for less than a week in the US, even though he says he knows he can't be with her. He finally admitted the affair was wrong a few weeks ago, which was a huge breakthrough, but he still seems stuck in a place of not being able to move toward truly reconciling with me."

I took a deep breath, staring out at the busy city street through the restaurant's glass walls.

"He now lives alone in a studio service apartment and has mostly isolated himself from our friends and community. His big thing is needing space to 'figure things out,' as he puts it, and he seems alive and inspired in some ways and also very down in others. He sees my counselor, which is great, but mostly in separate sessions from me. My communication with him is pretty limited."

Jody kept her intent gaze fiercely locked on mine.

"Corrie, I believe you and I are meant to pray together for you and for Chase. This prayer will not be like a prayer group, where we go around and pray for each other. No, this is just for you and for Chase and for things in your situation. How is Friday at eight p.m. for you?"

"You mean next Friday?" I asked.

She smiled. "Every Friday, as long as it takes. I will be here at eight p.m., and we will pray in the spirit."

I simply nodded my head slowly, totally floored by this offer.

And pray we did, every Friday night for the next two years. She stayed one to two hours each time. I always updated her on the latest with Chase and the pain as well as some of the beautiful things God was releasing in my life. We started with prayers of forgiveness toward Chase as a guard against bitterness and self-pity.

I remember her words about the arduous journey of forgiveness.

"Corrie, forgiveness is not letting someone off the hook. It's releasing them to God so God, in His justice, can go after their issues, not you. In his kindness, His relentless kindness, He will lead them to repentance. It's not up to you."

She would hold my hands and agree in prayer with me as I prayed:

"Chase did this (action). I choose to forgive him, even though it made me feel (emotion). I choose not to hold it against him."

Then she would affirm my identity.

"Lord, thank You that Corrie is first and foremost Your *bride*, Your beloved daughter. That as a bridegroom rejoices over his bride, so You rejoice over Corrie. That You and You alone have her heart first, and what the enemy means for destruction, You are redeeming and accomplishing Your character in her."

She taught me about spiritual strongholds—areas in our life oppressed by lies and darkness. For example, when Chase voiced suicidal thoughts to me, Jody and I prayed against the spirit of death, tearing down that stronghold in Jesus's name and declaring life and hope over him in its place.

We prayed for the woman he had the affair with, Rachel. We declared scripture that came to mind. We prayed the tie Chase had with this woman would be broken, that every time he thought of her, he would taste ash in his mouth. That Chase would be overwhelmed by the love of God and would truly repent and experience godly sorrow, leading to life and hope.

I stepped into more and more boldness as I learned to pray like Jody prayed. Not prayers to beg and plead with God but rather prayers full of faith and authority. As we prayed, we also listened, and things came to mind to pray that sometimes seemed odd.

For example, one Friday, Jody asked me, "Is Chase still smoking?"

I nodded. "Yes, every day, as far as I know."

"I sense that today we need to pray against the spirit of addiction over him."

So we did, and then a few days later, after a Tuesday joint counseling session, Chase turned to me, unprompted.

"I quit smoking, you know," he said in a matter-of-fact tone.

I sucked in my breath and asked him casually, "Really? When?"

"This past weekend," he replied.

"Oh, cool. What day, out of curiosity?" I asked.

He shrugged. "I don't know. I think it was Friday. Yeah, Friday night, because normally I smoke more over the weekend. So I just decided to stop cold turkey. It was time."

I nodded. "That's great."

I was jumping inside, a direct encouragement from God that our prayers were impactful, shaking things up in spiritual realms. Now, do I believe we can influence anyone's free will in prayer? No, but we can certainly push back the darkness over them so they can see truth more clearly and use their free will to choose the light.

Over the course of the two years, we saw God answer prayers in incredible ways, including seeing Chase experience continued breakthroughs. I was able to repent in prayer for unforgiveness, for submitting to fear, as well as for making Chase an idol in my life. I declared forgiveness into spiritual realms, asked for deep healing, and learned to listen for truth over me and receive it in Jesus's name.

Sometimes a picture or vision would come to mind during prayer with Jody, or I would share a dream with her that I or someone else had for me that week. And then we would pray into it.

For example, one week, I had a dream I came across a little seven- or eight-year-old boy playing in a room, holding up the end of a cord of an unplugged electrical appliance. The boy looked at me and simply said, "Chase is disconnected. He's just disconnected."

So Jody and I would pray something like "Lord, we ask You will show Chase how to reconnect with You, how to plug into his source, which is You. Speak to him, and open his ears so he can hear You."

Another week, I had a dream about Chase slow dancing with me in a kitchen. Chase's whole demeanor was kind, humble, and gentle in the dream, and he looked at me with clear eyes. I recognized this as God showing me His heart of what reconciliation looked like, a heavenly perspective. So Jody and I would pray and declare boldly, "Lord, let it be on Earth as it is in heaven!"

As this weekly prayer became a routine, I noticed my posture start to change. Instead of clutching my knees to my chest on the couch all the time, I was sitting or standing with alertness. I felt less like a victim and more like an active contender as I declared my prayers with authority. I was reading scripture out loud and feeling more and more comfortable and familiar with turning my attention and my mind's eye to the spiritual realm, especially when things felt stagnant or confusing in the physical realm.

Times in prayer with Jody were so encouraging for me that I naturally started finding opportunities to pray with others as well. I invited three other women from the church to pray with me at my apartment twice a month. With this new group, we focused on listening to God and praying over each other in turn, speaking out what we heard or saw. To both receive prayer as well as pray over others was so life-giving.

I felt drawn to pray more with friends during small group as well as for strangers at church on Sundays. Some weeks, it felt like my apartment was just a revolving door to a series of prayer warriors—some planned and some not.

I noticed I was less and less impacted by what Chase was or wasn't doing. Before, what he would say or not say would wreck me, but now I wasn't taking as many cues from him. I was learning to look up instead, doing my best to walk "according to the Spirit," as Jody would always say.

I recognized God had sent this prayer warrior as a catalyst to awaken the fierce prayer warrior in myself as I continued my journey of walking around the circle.

CHAPTER 13

A Pinprick of Light

"Lord, we ask that every time Chase thinks about what direction to go and what to do, every option around him would feel totally dark and black, like death, except for the idea of reconciling with Corrie."

Jody paused, and I continued, sitting up straight on the cream-colored couch.

"We pray when the thought enters his mind to reconcile with me, he would see light; that the path of reconciliation would be the only place he sees light."

By the middle of May 2011, Jody and I had been praying together for months, and I had learned to pray with precision and specificity. The February breakthrough with Chase had been a promising start, but he was still genuinely wrestling with how to fully let go of the relationship with Rachel and whether or not to reconcile with me.

My mind was still consumed with thoughts of Chase daily, and I was wrestling with the mountain of pain threatening to crush my spirit, save for the continued divine "11-11 moments" that kept popping up, as well as the encouraging prayer times with Jody and others.

My weekly or twice-weekly counseling sessions with Karim had continued to be a lifeline for me as well. Several days after this prayer with Jody, I walked slowly into his office and plopped down into the familiar overstuffed red chair in the corner, facing him with trepidation as I asked what I always asked first.

"Have you talked to Chase recently?"

Karim had been having individual sessions with both of us, and the way he functioned as a counselor, which we agreed to at the start, was that anything we shared during individual sessions, Karim could share with the other person, unless a particular piece of information was specifically requested to stay confidential.

He paused, looking back at me intently.

"Corrie, something fascinating has happened." Karim, as always, seemed calm in his demeanor, but today, his calmness seemed mixed with an intensity I didn't recognize as he started sharing. I hung on every word of his even-toned voice.

"Chase reached a very low place in the last few days. He told me in one of his darkest moments last week, he was thinking about how to move forward."

I spied an unmistakable twinkle in Karim's eyes as he leaned forward. I held my breath.

"He was lying on his kitchen floor in the dark, running through all the options in his mind. He told me every option, every path around him was dark, totally dark. But then, he thought again about the option of reconciling with you, and he started to see something different—a tiny pinprick of light. It was very faint, but he said it was the only light he saw."

He paused and then went on.

"During our session, he told me about this light, and somehow he knew he needed to follow it, even though he did not feel emotionally connected to the idea of reconciling at all. But it's the only light he sees. We had a good conversation, and I encouraged him to take a step toward the light. Yes, this is very fascinating."

"Karim, that was exactly my prayer." I sat there stunned, my eyes filling with tears.

He smiled a warm but cautious smile.

"Indeed. This is going to be a process, Corrie. I encourage you to take it very slow. Chase is still in a very unsure place. But he is going to try. If you're available tomorrow, I'd like to have a joint session at five p.m."

"Yes, of course. Thanks so much, Karim."

After the session, I walked toward my scooter in the parking lot and clipped my helmet on as I tried to further process this news. I exhaled deeply, my heart skipping with joy.

Should I call Chase or wait to see him tomorrow? What now? Oh my gosh!

I checked my watch and decided if I hurried, I could make it to Leanna's in time for dinner and share the news with her. Ten minutes later, I arrived at her apartment building and walked into the familiar lobby toward the elevator. It was empty and mostly quiet, save for the chatty Chinese commercials flashing on a little TV mounted on the wall above the "up" button.

I tapped my foot as I watched the numbers above the TV slowly descend. My heart raced with excitement as I exhaled a stream of thank-you prayers for Chase's breakthrough.

God, You're so amazing! You can literally speak through anything anywhere—through pinpricks of light, through angels, through nature… Gosh, if You wanted to, You could speak in an audible voice right now into thin air or even through this little TV.

At that moment, my gaze fell to the little screen, which was flashing a bank's name. Then came the background music, and my whole body froze. The elevator doors opened, but I couldn't move.

Really, God? Really?

I had only ever heard this song once in my life—seven years earlier on my wedding day. It was a classical piece by Rachmaninoff that Chase had specially picked out for me to walk down the aisle to. I just stood there, jaw open,

gasping, then starting to laugh… a deep knowing laugh…
just me and God.

"Now You're just showing off!" I said out loud as I pushed
the button again to open the elevator door, in awe of the
God whose heart was for my marriage. I marveled at His
orchestration of "11-11 moments" like this and knew I needed
to keep following Him.

Over the next few days, Chase and I had the joint counseling
session and decided to start spending more time together,
doing simple things like going to coffee. He still seemed
very emotionally distant and could not say "I love you," but
his tone was warmer toward me, and he reached out a little
bit more often.

I sensed this was really hard for him. He said he was just
trying to keep putting one foot in front of the other, moving
toward the light, and trusting somehow he would get there. I
felt confident he would. He texted me one weekend afternoon
to ask if he could come over with Dairy Queen ice cream. I
was thrilled.

"Of course." That was the first time he kissed me since
everything happened—another rush of reassurance.

A few days later, Chase invited me to dinner. After the meal,
we walked outside onto the dark street, and I spied a bench
glistening with raindrops under a flickering street light.

"Can we sit for a minute?" I asked. "I'd really like to pray."

He nodded, and we brushed the wetness off the bench with our hands as best we could. As we sat there in the humid city warmth, I put my hand on his back and started praying, our heads bowed.

"God, we need Your help to do this, to know how to walk forward. We need You."

Chase's shoulders trembled, and all of a sudden, his head shot up, as if being jerked awake. His eyes were wide, and he was literally gasping for air, taking huge quick breaths. He looked around like he was taking in his surroundings for the first time, then looked right at me and started to cry.

"What in the...? Oh my gosh! The hardness is gone. I'm sorry! I'm sorry. I'm so sorry for what I did. I miss you! I miss your family." Then he turned to me and grabbed my face in his hands. "I love you so much! I'm so, so sorry."

His eyes shone. They were clear. I hadn't seen those eyes in months. I hadn't heard "I love you" in longer.

There you are, Chase. Welcome back.

He buried his face in my neck and against my chest, and I held him there on that bench, rubbing his back in awe.

For the next few weeks, his eyes stayed clear. The way he described it in counseling was that the little nucleus of light he had seen in the darkness was growing and expanding. We still lived apart but started spending more time together.

Then came a gut-wrenching decision. He felt compelled not only to continue his PhD program but to go back in July and face "her" to say in person the relationship was really over. At first, this was laughable to me.

"Of course not, Chase! How, by any stretch of the imagination, is that a wise call, especially based on what had happened in January?"

I felt in my spirit I needed to stand my ground and say no, so I did. I was not okay with this. It felt good to stand firm when I had hardly ever done this with him in the past.

He argued back, insisting on this idea. But I refused and told him we could talk about it in counseling.

The next day, Karim heard Chase out and encouraged us to talk through the idea again but this time repeat back to the other person what we heard them say and then try to come to a decision together.

That night, Chase and I sat in our apartment and faced each other. I cried tears of sadness and hurt as I shared my major hesitations with his idea, how fragile my heart was, and how I still had no trust in him.

He was softer than the previous day somehow, and he took a breath and repeated my concerns back to me one by one. This type of exchange happened for over an hour, and as it did, my shoulders relaxed as I started feeling heard and acknowledged for the first time in a very long time. I asked if I could give him a hug.

"Sure," he said and leaned over to hold me. "Corrie, if you're truly not okay with me going then... I won't. I really won't."

I looked into his eyes. They were clear. He continued.

"Something in me just feels a need to face Rachel from a place of strength, to know I can, and to apologize for the pain I caused her and her husband. I truly feel this would help me move forward with you, and I just can't shake this idea of *needing* to see her, not even really wanting to but feeling compelled to."

I listened, voiced concerns, then listened again. Each time, he heard me, validated my perspective, and told me he would not push this on me but truly felt it would help him and us.

I felt a deep sincerity in him. I took a day to pray about it, and by the evening, I sensed the purpose in holding my ground had been accomplished. Chase was truly willing to not go.

We agreed to meet again the following day, and as I let him in the door of my apartment, I felt something had unlocked in me. We sat on the couch again, and I turned to face him.

"Chase, I prayed about it, and if you really sense it strongly from God, I will be okay with it."

We looked at each other and just blinked. I felt a strand of electricity between us, a sense of real partnership I hadn't felt in many months with Chase, or maybe ever. I didn't feel pushed to go Chase's way but instead felt respected and included in a way that was very new. The dark cloud of torturing images of him with "her" seemed to have temporarily lifted, and it was just me and my husband.

Our connection felt different and stronger, and the embrace that came in those next moments between Chase and me was full of light—a portal back to oneness God had opened up for us from just a pinprick of light, leading us lighted step by lighted step.

CHAPTER 14

But Even If He
Does Not

"Let's go on a trip when I get back from the States in August, like a second honeymoon. Where would you like to go?"

Chase's eyes twinkled as he voiced the question, and I felt like a little kid. It was early July, and he would be gone the latter half of the month.

"Normandy, France!" It was the place that first popped into my mind—a place I had been when I was younger and loved.

"Normandy it is!" he said, and he immediately started looking for flights and for places in the countryside to stay.

We made plans for how we would text and talk each day he was gone in the US and that he would keep me updated on anything with Rachel. We even cowrote an email that I watched him send to her, sharing his decision to reconcile with me. We decided he would not call her or arrange to meet up with her directly but would just wait to see if he happened to run into her on campus.

He packed his bags for his two weeks in the US, and in the meantime, he booked a beautiful old-fashioned hotel for us in the French district of Shanghai for our seventh anniversary. It was magical and also hard. Waves of pain and grief started hitting me at random times during the weekend. Though I had felt protected from them when we had first reconnected, they came up again—huge waves. And I didn't try to stuff them down like I had during the initial months of the crisis.

I expressed my pain when it came up. For example, we were at a restaurant for our anniversary meal, and he ordered a vegetarian option. As he closed his menu and handed it back to the server, a lightning bolt of pain surged through me. The other woman had inspired him to go cold turkey vegetarian last summer. Images assaulted my mind—him with her, him being with her, him being inspired by her. Then the sad, pitiful image of me—the "predictable," boring wife.

Tears stung my eyes and spilled down my cheeks as the server walked away after taking our order. Chase looked at me with compassion as I choked down a sob. I managed to force out the words, slowly.

"It was your order." I looked down. "I just get hit with these images of you with her. It hurts so much."

Without a word, he came over to my side of the table, sat down on the bench next to me, and slowly put his arm around me, pulling me close.

"I was such a jerk," he said. "I'm so, so sorry. I love you so much."

More quiet sobs came up as he held me. I felt seen, the truth seeping in bit by bit to those places inside me that were crushed and bruised from lies. For months, I had been healing and taking in truth from God, from others, and from scripture. But something felt accelerated when Chase was saying it. I could actually foresee what reconciliation would look like ahead—a painful but glorious process.

So much more pain needed to bubble up, and so many more places needed healing. But I knew it was a process, one step at a time. I was so grateful to really be reconciling, finally, and not on his terms but on both of our terms. We held each other long into the night of our seventh anniversary.

In the Pudong airport terminal the next day, he gave me a final hug, smiling as he turned to walk through security.

"I love you so much. I'll call you the second I land."

Fast forward a couple of days, I told my family I was allowing Chase to meet with "her," and they absolutely flipped out.

"What could possibly be wise about that, Corrie? He's setting himself up to do exactly what he did before."

I heard them out for hours, prayed about it more, and then respectfully disagreed. I understood their fear. I would have been terrified too if I hadn't felt the distinct seed of faith come in like it had that night I discussed things with Chase.

Later that week, in my Friday time with Jody, she grabbed my hands and stared at me intently.

"Both you and Chase have made the decision in faith, and God will honor that. I think it will be powerful for Chase to face her and declare he is choosing to stay married to you. In fact, I sense we should pray he would run into this woman on campus."

So we did. At that point, it had been over a week, and nothing. She was in a different cohort of students, and he hadn't seen her. He and I were talking every day, and things seemed good. Then came the last day he would be on campus. Jody and I prayed all day.

Let him run into her today.

I got a call from Chase in the evening.

"It's done," he said. I could hear the relief in his voice.

"Did you see her?"

"Yes. I was walking across the parking lot after my last class and ran into her. I asked her if she wanted to go to coffee, said I had some things I wanted to tell her. We went to coffee for thirty minutes or so, and I apologized to her for the pain I had caused her and her husband. I told her I was reconciling with you and hoped she was going to reconcile with her husband."

He went on to tell me the sheen was gone from her. She looked like a normal person to him, a person in great pain. She apologized as well and told him she was reconciling with her husband too.

"And that was it." I heard the relief again in his voice.

"Wow," I said. "We were praying today would be the day you would run into her. I'm so glad it went well and that you faced her."

Thank You, Lord.

We talked about him finalizing some details for France, wrapping up the final odds and ends of his classes, and packing to come home.

"See you tomorrow, love. I can't wait to see you," I said.

"See you tomorrow," he said.

When Chase came back to Shanghai, he was exhausted and still living in his service apartment.

When I finally saw him a day or two later, the light was out of his eyes. I can't think of any other way to describe it. The clarity I had seen and experienced for several weeks in July was gone, just like that.

"I'm having a lot of doubts," he said. "If I'm honest, I'm not sure it would be a good thing to go to France together right now. I need some time to think."

I was shocked. "We have our tickets and plans booked, babe. We're leaving in just over a week."

"I'll think about it," he said.

A day before the trip, he called me.

"Okay, I don't feel emotionally present, but I'll go to France with you. I'm going in faith, not because I feel like I want to right now."

I agreed, still shocked and confused. Where had our connectedness suddenly gone? He felt cold and distant.

So we went to France as planned, yet even in the beauty of the Normandy countryside, it was miserable between us. Chase was back to being distant and disconnected, as well as irritable and aloof.

When we arrived at the room at our picturesque bed and breakfast, he immediately walked over and put his pillow at the foot of the bed.

"We can sleep here, but I need to sleep this way, and you can sleep the other way," he said.

I swallowed.

He insisted on spending a lot of time on his own while he smoked and hid away to tinker on his laptop with photographs he had taken.

Despite this dynamic, we still managed to go out and explore a bit. We went to the Louvre Museum in Paris, listened to the haunting melodies of a cellist playing in the Mont-Saint-Michel castle, indulged in fresh raw oysters on the shore of

Cancale, and strolled through a market where I found the most delicious pear I'd ever tasted.

I did my best to walk in the hope God had revealed to me so many times—the reality of His heart to reconcile our marriage—and surprisingly found myself able to stay positive for much of the time.

But I felt utterly alone.

When Chase was doing his own thing, I would go on walks by myself, listening to music and crying out to God.

What is happening? Bring him back, God.

Chase hardly touched me the entire trip, not even holding my hand. On our last night, we went on a walk after dinner, and I just broke, asking him to try to describe where he was at and tell me what was wrong.

"Is it about her?" I asked.

"No, it's not," he insisted. "I'm truly done with her. I just realize I still have a lot of questions and doubts about God and Christianity, and just other questions about life I need to explore. I just need time to think, to figure things out."

We finished the walk and got back to the car. I felt sick. He had come back, and it had been beautiful.

"What do you need to figure out?" I pleaded with him. "Why can't we figure this out together, Chase?"

I gasped for air, tears and snot pouring from my face as I sobbed uncontrollably. There were no tissues, so he took off his white undershirt and handed it to me, a pinched look on his face. He just shook his head.

"I don't think I will ever change, Corrie. I honestly don't think I will ever be able to love you the way you need or be one hundred percent committed to you. I tried for those few weeks, and tried to overlook my remaining doubts, but they are still there and are big, even with her out of my life now. There are still issues with just us. We're so different, and we are going different directions spiritually."

He hesitated.

"This might be hard to hear, but… I honestly don't think I should have married you. Now that I know myself better, I would make a different choice, and I don't know what to do with that. It's all my fault. I just wasn't self-aware enough, and during our marriage, I hadn't dared to question it but did feel myself shutting down and needing to escape. Yes, I did feel a general spiritual connection with you before—not bad and not great. We are just so different, too different. I honestly can't imagine having kids with you."

I coughed, choking on my sobs as he went on.

"I feel God is giving me a choice: He would be okay with divorce, and He would be okay with me staying married to you too."

I was emotionally drained. I couldn't hear more. We drove in silence back to the bed and breakfast. He stayed outside to smoke. I crawled into bed and opened my Bible.

God, what do I do with this? What are You doing?

The pages fell open to Daniel 3, and dark, watery blotches appeared on the thin pages as I began to read. It was the story of the three righteous men Shadrach, Meshach, and Abednego, who had been summoned to appear before King Nebuchadnezzar before being thrown into the fiery furnace for refusing to worship the king's golden idol.

Furious with rage... Nebuchadnezzar said to them, "But if you do not worship it, you will be thrown immediately into a blazing furnace. Then what god will be able to rescue you from my hand?"

Shadrach, Meshach and Abednego replied to him, "King Nebuchadnezzar, we do not need to defend ourselves before you in this matter. If we are thrown into the blazing furnace, the God we serve is able to deliver us from it, and he will deliver us from Your Majesty's hand. But even if he does not, we want you to know, Your Majesty, that we will not serve your gods or worship the image of gold you have set up."

—Daniel 3:13–18[1]

"But even if he does not," I whispered the words as they seeped into my consciousness.

I felt frozen in time.

What if the worst is really going to happen? What if he decides to divorce me?

I knew there was no guarantee Chase would come back, but I realized how tightly I was still holding this outcome. Shadrach, Meshach, and Abednego had openly declared that although they were not sure about the outcome, they were sure about the truth of who God was. He was the true God, the only God, and the one who had the power to save them from physical fire. They were trusting Him regardless of the outcome.

I cried, holding my hands out in front of me, hands that had clung desperately to the outcome I felt I needed. With my palms facing up, I slowly loosened my fingers and realized I was still holding Chase's damp undershirt. It dropped to the floor. My palms were fully open now. I breathed out a brief declaration that resonated deeply within me, even as doubt lingered in some corners of my mind.

God, I trust You. The outcome is Yours.

The silence enveloped me—yes, the familiar stillness. I knew I was not alone as I curled up on my side of the bed for one final night in the preposterous arrangement with Chase's feet by my face.

My spirit was quiet as we packed the next morning, drove to the airport, and flew back home to Shanghai. Trying to reason any further with Chase was not going to help. The outcome was in God's hands now. Only He could lead Chase to genuine and sustained heart change, and Chase had to choose it for himself.

The taxi ride with him from the Pudong airport felt longer than normal. I thought back over the bizarre and miraculous summer, the life-filled steps Chase had taken back toward me, and how the door had closed again, his eyes distant.

God, why didn't he keep walking forward? Why is he walking away again?

I was devastated, yet I had noticed something about myself. Despite how beautiful the reconciliation process had been, in the secret place of my heart, I had felt myself downshift spiritually. I noticed a struggle with surges of the Noise again—feeling overwhelmed, scattered, apathetic, and second-guessing decisions at work.

I had lost my center focus, going right back to idolizing Chase while putting God back on the shelf. Falling back into this familiar pattern and disconnecting from God had been so easy. I contemplated whether I was ready yet for long-term reconciliation.

Could this be a kindness of God, giving me more correction, more time to learn how to change my source to Him, to stay tuned into Him?

Our taxi pulled up on the street corner at the gate to my apartment building. Chase helped me with my suitcase and gave me a pitiful half hug.

"See you later," he said in a strange tone, as if I were an acquaintance.

"See you later..." I whispered. He got back in the taxi and closed the door.

Okay, God. I surrender! Help me get back to being focused on You. I don't want to do life in any other way.

Chase was gone again. It was back to me and God.

CHAPTER 15

Leaps of Faith

Flipping channels one day, actor Jack Black's round and mischievous face popped up on my TV. It was his movie *Shallow Hal*, with Gwyneth Paltrow.

Oh no, I can't do romantic comedies.

For the entire year since everything had happened, watching any romantic theme on TV or in movies had felt gut-wrenching for me, so I had stopped watching most things altogether. It was early September, and I was still readjusting after the start-stop reconciliation process with Chase over the summer.

My prayer was that God would do the work needed in Chase's heart while he was "away" again, and my days were filled with the continued strange mixture of grief and joy as I put my focus on listening to God, experiencing "11-11 moments," and following His cues. Living alone was still so odd.

I could use a laugh today, God.

I cautiously let the movie keep playing, and to my surprise, I was able to enjoy it without bursting into tears. In fact, a warm feeling of closeness came over me, and I took a deep breath.

God, You're here with me. Thank You.

I laughed as celebrity motivational speaker and life coach Tony Robbins made his hilarious cameo appearance to hypnotize Jack Black and make him see only the inner beauty of women.

When the movie ended, I could not shake this feeling I needed to know more about Tony Robbins. I had heard his name but wasn't sure what his organization was about.

Is this weird curiosity from You, God?

I sensed a "yes" and even a kind of winsome nudge from God to look up his organization. Again, I was not the kind of person who searched for things online for fun, but there I was, scanning the Tony Robbins website and watching his introductory video. I noticed a big button for a free coaching session.

Why not?

With a sense of playful intrigue, like Alice following the white rabbit into Wonderland, I clicked the button and set an appointment for the following week.

When the day of the call arrived, a coach, Ben, appeared on the screen with fiery energy in his eyes. He explained he was their "placer" to do initial calls and then place people with the right coach if I wanted to move forward.

I shared my situation with him of being separated from Chase, praying for his return, and focusing on personal growth in the meantime. Energy sparked out of the screen.

"Corrie, can I be blunt?"

His tone was encouraging, and I nodded.

"It sounds like you are spending a lot of time and energy analyzing Chase, but the truth is, you can only control your own growth. Everything Chase is doing right now is based on his own needs, not yours." He paused.

"Right, but I do want to reconcile with him."

"Yes, but is that the reason you want to grow? Coaching is about growing to get to the next level, and your motivation needs to be crystal clear. My question to you is: Why *must* you grow? Who *must* Corrie be today to see the world from a new lens, regardless of what Chase does? What are Corrie's dreams?"

I paused, thought for a while, and then laughed. "You know, it's funny. I think I might want to sing more and explore my creative side, maybe paint, and maybe get a master's degree at some point. I'm always so productive and rarely do things just because I want to."

Ben smiled. "*Yes!* I love these ideas, Corrie. This growth I'm talking about is not so you can survive this crisis or find stability again. Your counselor has already helped with that, and you're in a stable place. Coaching is about leaping forward, creating success and significance in every area of your world. A coach will help you set goals and expand your psychology of who you are, what you are capable of doing, and how you are worthy of being treated."

My heart was beating fast. "Ben, I think it's time for that! I've been so focused on Chase, honestly kind of waiting on him to grow or to come back, before I really allow myself to grow. But you're right, I'm not in control of that. I want to keep praying for him, of course, but in the meantime, I think I can say I *must* discover and grow more in who I was created to be."

After the call ended, I started journaling, exhilarated.

"Wow, I'm someone without Chase! I'm someone! I have unique things to contribute! My needs can be met without Chase!"

It is hard to believe now this was largely a new thought to me at the time. Since day one of my crisis, it felt like I had been building a little campfire of autonomy and independence, but the call with Ben had just doused it with lighter fluid!

Signing up for a year of coaching was a big leap for me financially. I wasn't used to making big decisions without Chase, but I sensed the whole thing had been a setup from God—an important investment in my growth.

I needed to grow now, for me, and stop linking my identity, value, and growth to a person.

Ben placed me with a female coach based in the US named Lynette, a middle-aged woman of strong Christian faith who also happened to be a licensed therapist. I felt an instant connection with her and will never forget the assignment she gave me on our very first call.

"Corrie, is there anything in your apartment that still belongs to Chase?"

"Of course. The entire office is full of his stuff. I actually haven't dared to go into that room this entire year. That is the room where he used to talk to the other woman and email with her. It's too painful."

Lynette paused and then said, "It's time to clear out that room, Corrie."

Tears stung my eyes. "*What?* No, I can't. I can't go in there. Plus, I still believe he's coming back. I want to leave it so it's ready for him."

Lynette's tone was caring and firm. "Corrie, when Chase comes back, you can redo the whole apartment together for a new chapter of your marriage. You can even get a new apartment. That is for then. This is for now."

I hesitated, letting the idea sink in. "Okay, I can try. But what do I even do with his stuff? And with the room? I don't need it."

I couldn't see Lynette's face but knew she was smiling.

"That's the fun part. Let's make a plan. This is your first assignment. Tell me some of your favorite foods, a music album you love, and a candle scent that makes you happy."

"Why?"

"Because this is going to be a Corrie room, so even when you're cleaning it out, from the very beginning, it's going to feel like a Corrie room. It's okay if you don't know what it will be yet. That will come."

The plan took shape. I was to message my husband and tell him I would be leaving some boxes of the remainder of his stuff outside my apartment door on Saturday afternoon for him to pick up. Check.

Then I was to go get some big cardboard boxes. Check.

Then go to the nice international grocery store and get sesame bagels, cream cheese, and smoked salmon, my favorite meal. Check.

I picked out a beautiful lavender-scented candle and got a music mix ready. Final check.

Then Saturday morning came. I stood at the office door and leaned against it, choking back sobs. I held my breath and pushed open the door, inch by inch, like I was peeking into a cemetery.

The office was exactly as he left it. His Ikea desk was stacked with papers and books, and the dusty shelves held office supplies, more books, photography stuff, and knick-knacks. The black office chair stared at me, empty and haunting.

I just stood there, feeling the tears flowing down my cheeks as I faced the giant hole Chase's absence had left in my life—the sadness, the aching, the loneliness, the rejection.

Then Lynette's insistent voice rang in my mind. "When you open the door, remember you are on assignment."

I followed her instructions almost mechanically. I pushed play on my iPod, lit the candle, and took a bite of my smoked salmon bagel. I chewed slowly as the vibrant melody washed over me and the lavender fragrance stirred my senses.

I can do this. I have to do this.

I reached for a book and put it in a box, and then another one. Then a stack of papers and some pens—done. I was breathing and singing to myself. I couldn't help it. The song playing was "Light up the Sky" by The Afters, one of my favorites.

Three hours later, I looked around. Everything was out. I had even dismantled the desk and put the pieces in a box for Chase to deal with. I texted him his things were ready. Check.

Then I remembered the next part of my assignment—clean the room and make it shine. So I did, with vigor, as tears continued to flow. I scrubbed the floor, washed the window, and wiped down each of the walls. Check.

My next assignment was to go to the paint store to pick a color for the room's new purpose, but first I decided to sit down on the floor in the middle of the clean and empty space. The lavender candle flickered beside me as I leaned back on my hands and looked around.

What will you be, little room?

I paused and took a deep breath, feeling as if I'd entered a sudden beautiful mist. Ideas began to land on me, like tiny beads of water. This room needed to be redeemed, from being a place of secrecy and isolation and depression to a place of... faith, joy, healing.

Yes!

This could be the faith room, a place for me to paint, read, and spend time with God. The color? Deep turquoise blue.

That's it!

More ideas emerged from the mist. I could go to the outdoor art market and pick out some new paintings. I could move the comfy chair from the living room to the corner by the window. I could find a pretty white bookshelf and fill it with my journals, photo albums, and some other pretty little things.

A giggle came up like a little friend, turning quickly into a deep laugh that refreshed my soul.

This is going to be awesome!

The next few days were a flurry of activity and excitement. I figured out how to paint the room then filled it with the beautiful things I'd gathered, including three new paintings by a local Shanghai artist—vibrant lily pads in a spectrum of blues, oranges, and greens floating serenely on a river to beckon tiny boats hovering in the distance. I was elated with how the faith room was taking shape, but a finishing touch was still to come, one I could never have anticipated.

The idea of getting a treadmill had been popping into my mind. Strange. I was a member of two gyms, biked everywhere, and took walks around Shanghai all the time.

Why would I want or need a treadmill? Is this You, God?

It certainly didn't feel like an idea I would have. So I researched online a bit and saw some used ones for sale, over 2000 RMB (roughly $300)—very expensive for me at the time. Nothing stood out to me.

Okay, I'll just keep my eyes open.

A few days later, an email jumped out at me about a friend's moving sale. On the list was a treadmill. My heart leaped, and I called her... only 700 RMB (about $100)!

Is this for me, Lord?

Yes.

I laughed out loud and immediately arranged to pick it up with the help of two gracious guy friends. When we finally hoisted it out of the elevator then up the stairs to its new home, it perfectly filled the empty space in the middle of the faith room.

That first night, I lit candles, turned off the lights, queued up some worship songs and a Graham Cooke talk on my iPod, then walked for almost an hour. I sang as I listened. I laughed. I cried out my pain. I cried out my joy. I yelled "Amen!" I made weird faces, uninhibited. I touched the side bars with the tips of my fingers and closed my eyes as Graham's British voice filled the dark space with encouragement.

Wow. A little different than walking outside with red lights, honking cars, and avoiding dog poop. I felt focused, vitality coursing through me as I cried out to God, immersing myself in truth and getting filled up.

No more falling asleep while praying. What a brilliant idea.

When I finally switched the treadmill off, I knelt down and poured out my heart to God, feeling His closeness.

Thank You for this faith room, for the idea of a life coach and a treadmill. Thank You for helping me dream again and for making me someone, regardless of what happens with Chase.

As much as I loved the new room, it was still so strange his stuff was no longer in our—I mean... my?—apartment anymore.

A couple of weeks after setting it up, I was biking home from an event one day and just missing my husband. I hadn't seen him for over two months, ever since coming back from

France. We had texted a few times and talked once briefly by phone, but mostly about logistics with moving his stuff, nothing meaningful. I knew he was looking for a new apartment, and I wondered where it would be and if he had moved yet. It was so strange to not even know where he lived.

As I biked through a neighborhood not far from home, I was struck by a random thought.

Pray you will see Chase.

I felt caught off guard but intrigued.

God, that is definitely what I want right now. But how does this work?

Pray you will see Chase.

The thought would not leave me, and I decided to give it a go. Why not? And while we're at it, why not make it ultra-specific? We're allowed to pray bold prayers, right?

Okay, God. Sure. I pray I will see Chase. In fact, I pray I will see him right at the corner of Panyu Road and Xinhua Road.

It was the big intersection I was about to pass, coming up in two blocks. As soon as I voiced the prayer, I wanted to take it back immediately.

God, I don't want to be disappointed.

Pray you will see Chase.

Okay, okay, fine. I pray he'll be right at that corner.

As my bike approached, I willed myself to look at the corner. Dozens of Chinese pedestrians hustled to their destinations next to a long row of parked bikes. To my surprise, right in the very center of the corner, I noticed a foreigner—they are easy to pick out—bending over his scooter, maybe unlocking his back wheel.

I sighed.

Oh well, God. At least it was a foreigner.

At that moment, as my bike turned the corner, the foreign guy stood up from his bent position.

It was Chase, standing there by his bike, exactly in the place I had prayed to see him! He was looking in the other direction, so he didn't see me, but there he was, my beloved husband. My eyes blurred with tears as a sob burst out of me.

Oh God! Oh God! Oh God! I can't believe it.

Corrie, I have him.

Then I heard it again.

I have him.

I picked up the pace and flew down the wide and tree-lined Xinhua Road. My pedals raced to catch up with my heart pounding in my ears as I tried to process what had just happened—yet another "11-11 moment."

God, You're so real. Oh my gosh. Thank You, thank You, thank You. Chase is Yours. I'm sorry for trying to hold him so tightly. I trust You.

CHAPTER 16

Jazz

Sing in a jazz club before November 11.

The thought would not leave my mind—when I was at work, at home, in the gym. By now it was October of 2011, and for a couple of weeks, every time I turned my attention to God, the thought was just there, like an unwelcomed guest at the door of my mind, incessantly ringing the bell again and again.

Sing in a jazz club before November 11.

I was confused. I was journaling late one evening, sitting on the same spot of the couch where I had seen the vision the previous year of the turtle walking around the circle of a year. I remembered what I had heard that day.

Corrie, it's going to be a year. Ride this out with me. I am redeeming your marriage. Walk that way.

The words and circle picture had been fueling and focusing me each day since the dark weekend when everything had crashed. God had brought my husband back once, and I knew He was either going to do it again on November 11 or had something else amazing in mind while I continued to wait for Chase's return.

The year was about to be up. The end of the year of redemption—11/11/11—was coming, and I did not want to miss anything from God. But now, a jazz club?

Is this You, God?

Yes, I heard.

But I'm not a jazz singer! I don't even know any jazz songs… do I? I just sing backup in church sometimes. I'm a choir singer.

I pushed back, then hesitated. This felt more like a directive than just an idea. So I sat there with God one day on the chair in the faith room, took a deep breath, and contemplated this idea of singing.

Wait… If I'm really honest, I think singing is important to me, maybe more important than I realize. I think, deep down, I actually might want to sing in front of and over people.

There it was, exposed and strange to admit, a secret I had hidden from my husband and even from myself. I blushed as I remembered the secretive singing sessions I used to have in my middle school bedroom—just me with my frizzy hair, braces, wired microphone, and double cassette boombox recording myself with the karaoke track of "Hero" by Mariah Carey.

I remembered the song I wrote in eighth grade for me and my friends to sing at our class graduation and how I gave away the solo parts to others, not wanting to draw attention to myself.

I remembered overhearing my California high school singing coach talking to our choir director.

"Of all the students, there are only a couple of them who stand out to me. One of them is Corrie. Her voice has really strong potential."

Still, I had shied away from solos and leading. When I met Chase, I looked to him as the confident worship leader and was happy just to harmonize and sing backup for him.

Even getting a small music scholarship in college had not convinced me to step out from the ensemble except for my mandatory solo recital, after which all I did was critique myself for my many mistakes. The fearful reasoning in my head had always gone something like: *Will other people think I'm trying to show off my voice? I won't be good enough for a solo anyway. Maybe someday I will, but I would need to practice much harder in my voice lessons so I could be "the best."*

On a family vacation once, I had gone out on a limb and signed up to sing "Eternal Flame" on stage at a karaoke event. My voice had distinctly cracked on the high note singing "flame," and it was all I could think about for weeks afterward.

Gosh, Corrie, you really screwed that up and embarrassed yourself.

But here I was now, at twenty-nine years old, and something about my crisis had eliminated pretense from my life. My whole world was falling apart, and I didn't really care anymore about what others thought. I didn't feel the need to please them anymore or worry about their perception of me.

I had also just started singing alone in the faith room in recent days as I walked out my pain on the treadmill. Music was becoming a powerful medium for me to connect with God and express my deep pain, my longing, and the deepest parts of myself.

The terrifying thought came again.

Sing in a jazz club before November 11.

God, that's such a crazy thought! Yet... kind of exhilarating, fun. And You know what, why the heck shouldn't I sing in a jazz club? What do I even have to lose?

So the next day, I told my life coach. I started telling friends, even random people I met. Why not?

"One of my current goals is to sing in a jazz club by November 11." Just a fact, as if it were really going to happen, which of course it wouldn't.

People flipped. They thought it was a great idea, brilliant! They threw out suggestions, connections, and real possibilities for how it might work.

Then I discovered it—a weekly open mic night on Sundays at a local jazz club called The Melting Pot.

Oh, God! It could really happen!

I found myself walking toward what I sensed was His voice, taking small, shaky steps of faith. I felt terrified, but it was the kind of terror I sensed He wanted to conquer in me.

Just trust me, Corrie.

I was much too intimidated to scope out the club by myself, so I called my prayer mentor, Jody, who was thrilled to accompany me.

The club was moody and dark, smelling faintly of cigar smoke and musty antiques. Deep red curtains with golden tassels adorned the navy walls, giving the room a classy mystique. The couches were the same deep red and slouched atop the dark hardwood floors, leading to a small, raised stage.

The four musicians were foreigners and played keyboard, double bass, and drums—a simple setup with a powerful output. My racing pulse slowed a moment as the sound of the room reverberated around me. The jazzy instrumental melodies riffed off each other in a playful dance.

It was still early evening, so the club was largely empty.

"Oh, this is it, Corrie! This is going to be great!"

Jody's distinctive warm and raspy voice was drowned out by my thoughts.

Will I really be able to get up on that stage next week? Those are professionals!

We asked a passing server how the open mic night worked. He explained how I just needed to choose from the songbook—he pointed to it on a side table—and then write the title on a small piece of paper and hand it in so they could call me up on stage when it was my turn.

The songbook was a massive black binder, and I perched on one of the red couches with Jody to flip through the pages, scanning rapidly for anything I knew. Some of the titles looked vaguely familiar, but only one stood out—"Stand by Me." I had heard it and could maybe do that one.

"Okay, Jody. Let's get out of here!"

I fled to the safety of my apartment, and later that night, I sat trembling as I pushed send at the bottom of the email I had willed myself to write. I had decided to just go for broke and invite all my friends and close colleagues, trying to play it cool.

"This Sunday night, 10:00 p.m., I will be fulfilling a dream (which has been on my heart to do before mid-November) and will be singing at an open mic night at a jazz club in Shanghai… Is it really real? Yes! Okay, it will just be a song or two, but still! Whoever can make it, you are more than welcome to come. Yikes! It's scary but cool… Thanks to all of you for the ways you have supported and encouraged me this past year!"

The date was set—Sunday, November 6, 2011—just five days before the November 11 deadline.

Okay, God, I will obey You. I will trust You. This is my journey with You. But I still don't really get it. Why a jazz club? Why now?

That Friday, one of my Chinese coworkers asked me which song I would be singing. I looked it up online to show her, and the first site that popped up had a top section explaining the origin of "Stand by Me." It said the lyrics were based on an old spiritual song from the Bible—Psalm 46. I gasped.

"My Psalm," I whispered under my breath.

My eyes glistened, and my voice cracked with emotion as I read it out loud to her.

God is our refuge and strength, an ever-present help in trouble. Therefore, we will not fear, though the earth give way and the mountains fall into the heart of the sea, though its waters roar and foam and the mountains quake with their surging...
                                        —*Psalm 46:1–3*[1]

Of course. There You are, Lord. You really are in this.

That's all I needed.

Sunday came. I entered The Melting Pot and was shocked to see the dark red room brimming full with over forty people. Almost all of them were *my* people who had decided to show up... *for me*. I was floored.

Midnight was approaching, and the nerves surged in my body as the MC called my name. I wiped beads of sweat from my lip and tried to walk up to the stage much more confidently than I actually felt. A cheer rose up from my friends.

You're going to screw it up, Corrie.

I shook off the invading thought as I gripped the mic with shaking hands.

Then the music started, and I just started singing.

The shift I felt that very moment was like a light turning on. *Flash!* My nerves immediately vanished. It happened so quickly that I just stood there, shocked.

Oh my gosh, I'm home. I love this! I know what to do.

I felt completely at ease, inviting everyone to sing along as my voice rang out, clear and strong.

This is me! This is what I do. This is what I was made to do.

After the first chorus, I started calling out musician solos, as if I'd been performing for years.

"Take it away on the keys!" I yelled to the keyboard player. He smiled and launched into an intricate solo. We all watched his fingers flying, mesmerized.

"Let's hear it for the keys!" I called out to the crowd. They roared with applause.

Next up was the drummer, then the bass player, and then back to the final chorus.

The fear had disappeared completely, and I didn't care what people thought of me anymore. I was captivated by the room, making the experience fun for everyone while singing out to the God whose brilliant idea this had been in the first place.

I finished the song with hand cues to the band for a dramatic, slow ending—I'd always seen singers do that.

The drums crashed and brought the song to a dramatic end as people cheered and rushed toward me. They covered me in hugs and even bouquets of flowers.

It was a moment in time I will never forget—one of the most exhilarating nights of my life.

Singing, especially in front of large groups, felt like a seed God planted in me before I was born—a seed I'd always known was there but had never allowed to flourish. That night, the seedling burst from the soil and started to fiercely grow. I was doing what I was created to do.

From then on, I nurtured the little sprout with a newfound confidence. I started solo singing at weddings and events as well as leading the worship team at church. I came to understand the power of music and singing to access the spiritual realm and the power of worship to cut through lies of the enemy.

CHAPTER 17

11/11/11

I knew God had something special for me on 11/11/11, but I never could have guessed I would stumble upon it in the line to the ladies restroom.

On the Friday five days after my jazz club experience, I was set to go to a leadership conference and was full of anticipation.

As I rode the subway toward Pudong, the eastern part of the city, I thought back to the comical and hopeful turtle picture God had brought exactly one year earlier when I was paralyzed on the couch and hearing Him tell me:

Corrie, it's going to be a year. Ride this out with me. I am redeeming your marriage. Walk that way.

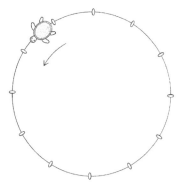

Throughout the past year of walking with God, I had started to see what He was doing under the surface. He wasn't just scheming to give me my husband back, though I believed that was still on His heart. He was drawing me into a more intimate relationship with Him, one that required turning to Him instead of my security blankets to mute the Noise.

He was teaching me to contend for the redemption of my marriage while at the same time handing over the outcome to Him. Holding these two ideas simultaneously was a challenge in that they could seem contradictory at times. But He was giving me faith to walk this way, so I did.

There had been the miraculous month-long reconciliation period over the summer and then Chase leaving as suddenly as he had returned. Chase's presence in my life was clearly not certain. Yet as my relationship deepened with the God of the Universe, I was coming to know His presence in my life as indisputably certain.

I finally arrived at the conference center and sat alongside several hundred other foreigners, all of us eager to hear from

God. While the content was impactful, nothing was jumping out as something special just for me.

When we broke for lunch, I made a beeline to the ladies restroom only to see a long line already snaking out the door. I went walking down a couple of side hallways in search of another restroom and finally spotted a small one tucked away in a nonconference area. Only two others stood waiting, and as I took my place in line, the girl just ahead of me caught my eye briefly and then turned to face forward. I noticed her short brown hair, casual jeans, and cloth bag across her shoulder.

A minute passed, and she glanced back at me, quite noticeably. She slowly turned around, looked down for a second, and then back up.

"Hi," she said hesitantly. "Do you... have a second to talk?"

"Sure." I smiled, curious, thrown a bit off guard by her demeanor.

"It's strange," she said. "But... I just had this sense when I saw you that we needed to meet. I'm Allie."

"Okay," I replied, always comfortable meeting new people but still curious. "Nice to meet you. I'm Corrie. Are you working here in Shanghai or studying?"

Her reply was careful and measured. "I'm... a college student here with a study abroad program."

I asked her which one and then gasped. It was the program Chase was leading that I used to heavily be involved in prior to our separation. My heart was racing.

"Oh my word, I know that program well," I said and then paused. "Allie, your director, Chase, is actually my husband."

We stood there staring at each other with a strange sense of mutual inner knowing. I also felt an immediate affection for this girl. I had so missed operating in my role as director's wife and getting to know the students, especially mentoring the girls.

"Yeah," Allie replied, weighing her words. "I heard he was married, but he just mentioned he was separated and hasn't talked about it other than that. I'd never seen your picture but had heard your name. And now... I think I'm... supposed to know you. It's really good to meet you, Corrie."

"It's good to meet you too, Allie. Part of me wants to skip the rest of the conference and just hear your story."

She brightened. "I would actually love that. I would love to hear yours too."

"Great," I replied as we reached the front of the restroom line. "Let's finish up our business here first for a minute though."

We laughed as we each found a stall and then we met up in the hallway to find our way out of the conference center. We went to dinner at a nearby restaurant and then on a night walk along the surrounding city streets. We talked for more than three hours, and the moments felt slow, beautiful, and rich.

Allie was the most mature twenty-year-old I'd ever met, a creative soul, and one who hadn't really found her place yet in the study abroad program. I shared with her parts of my journey with God over the previous year, including how significant the 11/11/11 day was to me. She was captivated. So was I.

"Allie, I really sense it was God's arrangement and gift to put you on my path today!"

"Likewise, Corrie." Her gaze was steady now.

Our friendship had begun, and we started meeting regularly for coffee until her semester ended several months later in April. I guess you could say I mentored her that year, but as I look back, she was also mentoring me, especially about being creative. I had started thinking about writing down some of my experiences with God, and as it turns out, Allie was a creative writing major, full to the brim with wisdom in that area.

I remember the twinkle in her gray-blue eyes when we met up for coffee one final time before she left Shanghai. She handed me a small, printed booklet of China stories she had written, complete with a red card stock paper cover.

"If you have time, I turned some of my journals into a little book," she announced.

"Wow, Allie. You just... wrote a book? That's huge. Thank you."

"It's no big deal," she said. "I hope you enjoy it."

Allie's book was a collection of brilliantly detailed stories about living in China—hilarious and poignant, recounting mishaps at indoor vegetable markets, attempted conversations with Chinese shopkeepers, and travel adventures in rural fishing villages. Her descriptions were vivid and lively, and I savored every page.

With all my fear-driven childhood baggage, sitting and enjoying a book just for fun was so rare for my hyperproductive self. But this was a new season, and Allie's friendship and passion for writing inspired my own inner creativity. Creative expression became a healing balm and a release valve for my pain.

I not only started reading for enjoyment, but in the months after meeting Allie, I also started my own writing project in a blog I called *Purple Phoenix Journey*. This outlet helped me process all the "11-11 moments" I was having with God as well as share my journey with others. I even pulled out the set of paints and easel Leanna had given me. In the stillness of the faith room, I painted the dreams and visions I was receiving from God onto huge sheets of white paper. All of this brought so much joy.

I marveled at the way God, despite Chase's actions and our separation, orchestrated a connection between me and one of the precious students from his program I had missed so much. It was a beautiful, redemptive 11/11/11 gift from my Creator.

Was it the gift of a redeemed marriage I longed for? No, it wasn't. I sensed this was still prominently on God's heart, but He also appeared very focused on my personal healing and kept revealing Himself to me in unexpected places.

Had I gone to the conference expecting to hear from God only through one of the speakers on stage, I would have missed encountering Him through Allie. I reflected on some of my experiences from the year—my experience at the jazz club and my interaction with Duyi and his mother, for example. As I did, I recognized how each day for me was beginning to unfold as a new adventure filled with divine surprises.

My obsessive focus on Chase coming back to me was shifting to pure anticipation of what God was doing.

What gifts are next, Lord?

CHAPTER 18

The Year of Corrie—Part 1

"Corrie, what if the coming year, 2012, were called 'The Year of Corrie'? What would that look like?"

At the end of 2011, just over a year into my crisis, my life coach, Lynette, was proposing an idea.

"What do you mean?" I asked, not fully understanding her question.

She went on. "What dreams do you have? Not for you and Chase, but just for you. Don't worry about whether they feel realistic to you or not. What would be fun for *you*? What would *you* love to do this next year, if you could? Wild ideas welcome."

I sat for a minute. What an odd question. I still wanted my husband to come back and restart the reconciliation process, of course. But by this stage, I had worked really hard to keep releasing my desired outcome to God's timing and plan and not try to control it.

I focused back on her question. *The Year of Corrie...*

"Hmm... I don't know."

A second later, three hilarious and wild ideas landed in my mind, like birds on a perch.

"Wild ideas, Lynette? Like anything?"

"Yes," she replied.

I felt like a little kid with a Christmas wish list.

"Okay, sure. Here goes. I want to go to a tropical place in Southeast Asia with my friend Kerri and learn how to scuba dive with her before she gets married this summer."

I giggled.

"Then I want to meet one of my favorite speakers, Graham Cooke, and shake his hand. Why not?"

I paused, thinking.

"Lastly, I want to have an eighth-grade reunion with all my childhood friends from my little private school. I was the eighth-grade class president, in fact, and it would be only right for me to help people reconnect now that we're all turning thirty this coming year."

I laughed again. "Ha, that was fun. Those are some crazy ideas for you, Lynette."

I'll never forget her response. "Corrie, those ideas don't sound crazy at all! They sound fabulous! How about you start looking into making them happen?"

What? I thought this was just an exercise!

But in that moment, a sudden energy struck me, the same type of adrenaline rush as when I was running around Shanghai collecting decorations and turquoise paint for the faith room.

Let's do this!

The moment I hung up with Lynette, I dialed Kerri's number in the States, and she picked up. I was ecstatic.

"Kerri! Okay, so don't freak out, but I have a crazy idea, part of this 'Year of Corrie' thing my life coach is having me do, and…. Well, this idea came to mind immediately. I just got an end-of-year bonus from my job, and I want to use it to fly you out here and go scuba diving somewhere in Southeast Asia. I'm totally serious. Would you be down?"

She laughed. We both laughed… hard. It felt amazing.

"Oh my gosh, Corrie! I would love that. *Really?* I think I actually might be able to pull it off with my schedule in late January. That would be incredible!"

She was in an interim job for a few months prior to her wedding and had some flexibility. And I really had just received an unexpected and very generous bonus from work that could easily cover the whole trip and her flight. I was freaking out.

Yes!

We quickly made plans in the following weeks to travel to Bohol, a small island in the Philippines. Leanna had told me about an affordable family-run resort there called Ravenala.

"When James and I first arrived there a couple years ago, I just stood and stared at the overwhelming beauty and cried," she had told me.

A natural, tropical setting was always a refreshing change from the concrete jungle and gray skies of Shanghai, but this place, according to Leanna, was extremely unique.

That did it for me. I took Leanna's word for it and called a travel agent to book our stay. When the confirmation email came, I noticed the name of my travel agent's company—Royal Light Travel—was located in room 1111 of the Commerce Spirit Building in Shanghai. It made me smile.

Thank You, Lord.

I felt like royalty as I made these plans, experiencing a continuous string of "11-11 moments."

When Kerri arrived at Shanghai's Pudong airport, she carried not only a massive roller suitcase for me filled with items not available in China but also an infectious energy that felt like a warm gust of air in my otherwise freezing city. She had been a roommate and sorority sister in college, part of the same tight-knit group of friends seeking God together since our freshman year. She was also the maid of honor at my wedding.

"I cannot believe this is really happening!" I said as we exchanged a joyful hug.

After taking two days to show her around Shanghai, we set off on our adventure—a flight from Shanghai to Manila, another flight from Manila to Cebu, a ferry from Cebu to Bohol, and then a two-hour bumpy van ride from Bohol to the tiny Ravenala resort.

I remember the softness of the grass under our feet as we stepped out of the cramped van and took in the scene in front of us. The resort was a lush secret garden with a canopy of palm trees spreading out across a brilliant green carpet of grass that glowed under the warmth of the sun. Giant tropical plants with fiery red and pink hibiscus flowers swayed in the light breeze as if to hail our arrival. A floral fragrance filled our lungs and enveloped our weary bodies in a sudden calm.

"Can you believe this, Kerri?" I squeaked with glee. It was ethereal.

As our driver helped with our bags, Kerri ambled over to the base of a thin-trunked tree with long, shiny green leaves and prominent clusters of white blossoms. I followed her, curious.

"It's plumeria," she whispered, a sense of awe in her voice. She reached down to pick up a flower that had fallen to the grass. It was shaped like a perfect upside-down trumpet. As she held it up to me, I noticed five exquisite white petals encircling a burst of radiant golden yellow at the center.

"This was my mom's favorite flower," she said as we both took turns inhaling the intoxicating fragrance.

I had known and loved her sweet mother, Pam, who had grown up in Hawaii and recently passed away after a long battle with cancer. I picked up another blossom, and we each put one behind our ears as a bright-eyed middle-aged lady, the "mama" of Ravenala, came to greet us and show us to our little bungalow.

"Welcome! I'm Teresita," she said warmly.

She and her family made us feel like family for the five days we spent in Bohol. She helped us arrange a four-day intensive scuba diving course at a PADI certification center nearby, roasted fresh fish and shrimp and rice for our daily dinners, and brought us endless homemade pineapple smoothies that tasted like heaven.

When we showed up at the nearby pool to take our first scuba diving lesson, I did a double take.

Chase?

The scuba instructor, Mason, bore a striking resemblance to Chase. He was similar in age, height, build, and even dark blond hair color and intensely blue eyes. Kerri noticed as well. She had been close friends with Chase and me in college.

Over the following days, as we spent hours with Mason training in the pool and doing short practice dives, Kerri and I both noticed something very distinct about him. He was gentle and kind, like a big teddy bear. We both felt safe with him, which was, of course, a very good thing since our lives were literally in his hands.

After studying for our written scuba tests and being in the water all day, Kerri and I were exhilarated and would have meaningful talks long into the night. We would talk about her mom, about grief, about Chase, and about her upcoming wedding. On our second to last night, we lounged in our lawn chairs on the moonlit beach. As we stared up at the stars, we enjoyed the soothing chorus of tropical frogs hiding in the trees.

"Mason is so kind," I remarked, sighing.

Kerri smiled. "He's also super attractive," she said, and I smacked her playfully on the shoulder.

This was certainly true, and I had to admit it was wonderful and slightly maddening to be around a guy like Mason in such close physical proximity for hours each day—in our swimsuits, no less. We were regularly peeling our wetsuits on and off, and his hands would constantly brush against me as he maneuvered my scuba gear and helped me clip it on and off for each session. Since the day Chase left, I had longed for physical affection and intimacy, sometimes frustrated beyond what I felt I could bear!

Thinking about my marriage and early crisis months with Chase, it struck me anew how focused we had been on Chase's needs over my own. To now be around a guy who was attentive to me and made me feel safe and cared for felt so refreshing. The fact both guys looked so similar made Mason's kind demeanor stand out even more.

"What a gift this experience is, Corrie. Mason seems to be such a tangible reminder for you of what simple kindness from Chase would feel like," Kerri remarked.

"I totally agree. Kindness is such an attractive quality, something I really want and need in my marriage moving forward, or really... just in my life in general, whatever happens."

Little did I know, the pinnacle of our Bohol adventure was yet to come. On our fourth and final day of scuba certification, we geared up for two deeper dives by a renowned section of the reef.

"The place we're going is known for its sea turtles," Mason told our small group, and I squealed with joy. Kerri gave me a knowing glance, as I had told her about the vision of the turtle going around the circle, of course. The year 2012 was a new year with new possibilities.

Mason went on. "I know where the turtles hang out, but sometimes we don't see them. Let's see if we get lucky today."

I prayed as the boat coasted closer to the dive spot.

God, are You going to bring me a sea turtle?

As I stepped off the boat with a splash, I felt the cool embrace of the ocean. I submerged into the deep blue, clearing my ears in regular intervals as we had been trained to do and releasing my air valve to go down and down. When we all reached fifty-five feet, Mason made the signal to stop descending. I pressed a bit on my scuba mask to secure it around my eyes and then blinked in wonder at the paradise surrounding me.

The sparkling coral shelf of magnetic colors seemed to beckon me forward, sea anemones and plants reaching out curious arms in my direction. A shock of neon yellow burst from under the shelf to my right—a glittering school of narrow fish, like tiny pencils darting around in a coordinated group. To my left, a striped neon blue and yellow fish the size of my hand flexed its body back and forth as it mingled with the plants, soon joined by a rainbow of other swimming creatures.

Mason had brought down a bag of condensed bread balls for the fish and motioned us over to release several pieces at a time to a swarming mob of dozens, who instantly gobbled them up. After one such feeding, the mob of fish cleared away to reveal just Mason in front of me making a "look up" gesture with his hand, followed by placing one hand on top of the other with his thumb and pinky flapping—the "turtle" gesture!

My eyes darted up as a massive sea turtle soared slowly above us, silhouetted by the rays of sunlight streaming in from above. My heart leaped as I watched it swim down to our level, right in front of us. Instinctively, my fins began moving, and I followed the sea turtle for a short distance, leaving the other divers behind and slowly kicking to position myself in perfect viewing range.

This is the most beautiful creature. Thank You, God!

The turtle's green shell was marked like a soccer ball with thin white lines and ridges that glowed turquoise in the blue ocean. Its extended head and slowly flapping arms were speckled green with their own more intricate web of glowing turquoise markings. I was mesmerized.

It was about fifteen feet below me now, and I found myself spreading out my arms and legs to mimic its movements, moving my limbs in slow motion exactly in sync with the turtle's. We floated and moved together, that sea turtle and I, and everything immediately slowed down—my thoughts, my breathing, my movements. The turtle's energy was a peaceful calm. There was not a hint of haste, just deliberate, trusting enjoyment.

I recognized this stillness. I was getting to know it very well.

This is how I want you to do life, my love, I heard in my spirit.

Every cell in my being felt alive and soothed by the presence of my Creator.

You're here.

Yes. I'm always here.

For a full minute, maybe even two, I continued to move in sync with the sea turtle below me, engaged in its serene, prayerful, slow-motion dance.

I want to do life like this, God. Trusting You, following You, moving with calm confidence, just like this. It's so peaceful.

I finally had to turn back to the group, and as we rose slowly to the surface, I knew a layer of healing had happened within me in that magnificent deep blue world. I was seen by the God of the Universe. He was beckoning me forward, captivating me with the spiritual realm, a realm that felt remarkably similar to the ocean. I wanted to be fully immersed in this realm, His realm—one of wonder, awe, peace, trust, and stillness.

"That's how I want to do life," I told Kerri as we celebrated our scuba certification that final evening under the stars.

She was finishing her last sip of yet another homemade pineapple smoothie from Teresita. Then she nodded and said, "We could not have planned a better grand finale for our trip."

Dream number one for "The Year of Corrie"—*check*!

Little did I realize how the timeliness of this beautiful, life-giving trip would prepare me to face what was coming just a few days later.

CHAPTER 19

The Letters

"Is your husband named Chase?"

The week after my trip to the Philippines with Kerri, an acquaintance of mine from work, Eve, approached me outside my office, speaking in a hushed tone.

"Yes," I said. "Why?"

"Are you still married?" she asked.

"Yes, but we've been separated for just over a year now. I haven't spoken to him in months," I said.

Eve winced. "I really don't want to meddle at all, Corrie, but I was cheated on once in a former marriage, and I would have wanted someone to tell me if they had known about it."

My body went cold with dread as she went on.

"I have a British friend here, Kara, who started dating your husband a few weeks ago."

I was speechless.

"She has been super excited about it. She keeps texting me to tell me how amazing he is and all about their relationship. He told her he's divorced, and just the other day, she told me he gave her a key to his apartment. I recognized his last name was the same as yours, so I had to ask and let you know, even if it costs my friendship with this girl."

She held up her phone and showed me the text messages. I felt instantly sick to my stomach.

"Thank you for telling me," I managed, my voice starting to shake. "I really appreciate knowing."

The next week was a blur. Eve gave me Kara's number so I could call her directly. When she picked up, I introduced myself and let her know Chase was married. She told me she knew and insisted Chase was just a platonic friend letting her keep some of her things at his place while she was in between apartments, hence the key.

After hanging up with Kara, I called Chase to confront him. He was livid I had called her and also insisted it was just a platonic friendship.

"Then why did you tell her you were divorced?" I asked.

"This is going toward divorce anyway, Corrie!" he said angrily. "I'm going to pursue a divorce."

The words struck me like arrows piercing my chest. I was so shaken by the intensity of his rage that I rushed to the door of my apartment to make sure it was locked, wondering if he still had any of his keys.

Then came my anger, red heat flushing through my body. I hadn't known how to access or even allow myself to feel this anger before because my terror of Chase leaving had left no room. Yet something had shifted in me. I wasn't terrified anymore.

Now the anger surged up from deep inside me. I was angry about Chase's affair with a married woman with kids, angry I'd been blindsided by rumors of his relationship—platonic or not—with Kara, angry he'd told her he was divorced, angry he'd blocked out most of the people who loved him the most, and angry he hadn't reached out to me in the six months since France to attempt to talk and work things out. Mostly, I was angry and hurt he seemed to keep throwing all my grace and forgiveness back in my face.

I texted him to let him know I would like to have a joint counseling session to talk about next steps, and he agreed. We arranged with Karim to meet that Saturday, February 4. The night before the session, I stayed up all night writing Chase a letter. My heart and tears gushed out like a raging waterfall onto all nine pages. Each page was full of my anger, my love, and my forgiveness, along with more than a few helpful curse words. I felt devastated yet fiercely alive as I wrote each page, spilling out my heart and continued hope for reconciliation.

I arrived at Karim's familiar office the next morning without having eaten or slept. Even still, I was ready. I wanted to fully express my heart to Chase. Karim asked me to read the whole letter out loud. It began:

"Dear Chase, I will never be able to fathom how you cannot see the value right now of what you have. The value of what you're being offered. The power of the redemptive process that awaits us if we choose to embark on it together. How can you not see it? How can you be so blind? I feel like you did see it once. You did taste it with me."

I went on.

"You'd rather convince yourself you never should have married me. That somehow, you not being fully self-aware— as if you are now—made the covenant invalid or something. 'Oops, sorry I screwed up. Shoot, Corrie, this was all a big mistake…'

"You know, as if the most loving thing you could do for me would be to divorce me. How noble. Divorce a woman who is 100 percent committed to you, who is for you, who wants to see you grow, thrive, become the person God has designed you to be."

About halfway through, I got to this part.

"[My love for you] wasn't perfect, and it still isn't perfect. But it's real, and it's not just from me. It is from God. How else could I forgive you for all that you've done? *I have forgiven you*, Chase. I choose to love you. I choose not to hold it against you."

It took me over an hour to read the full letter. I sobbed as I read. I shouted some parts and whispered others. I was fully myself, holding nothing back. I remember Chase looking down as he listened, and Karim's face wet with tears. I ended with this:

"I have a counter proposal for you than your scared and childish desire for divorce: You and I spend the next six months 100 percent full force making this work. And if at the end of the six months, it doesn't work, and if either one of us feels that, then we go our separate ways. Are you man enough to do that? Are you man enough to try? I love you. He is for us."

I folded the letter and just looked at Chase, my eyes fiery with passion. He looked tired and said nothing. Karim jumped in.

"Corrie, what you just shared was incredibly important and powerful. It was also a lot. Before Chase responds, I have an idea for what might be a good next step. How about we end this session now and reconvene tomorrow for a second joint session, and Chase can have a chance to write you something tonight and share it with you tomorrow?"

Chase nodded.

"Can I give you a hug before we leave, Chase?" I asked.

"Of course," he said.

I hugged him right there in front of Karim. I hugged him because I loved him, even though the hug felt more like I was hugging an acquaintance. I missed my Chase. I knew the kind and loving person God had created him to be, and I was truly baffled about why he was still walking away.

"See you tomorrow," I managed.

The following day, I sat next to Karim this time, and Chase faced us with a letter he had typed up. His tone was solemn and sincere.

"Corrie, I start writing this, knowing I will not likely be able to put all, or even most of it, into words and language that are clear yet. And although I may not be able to do so at this point, I hope you can hear my heart throughout and my desire to lay it openly and honestly before God and you."

He talked about not wanting to try to defend his decision to divorce but to help me understand more where he was coming from. The letter continued.

"I am not running away in this decision. I am consciously, and ironic as it may sound, sincerely walking forward toward God in the only way I can.

"I believe God is capable of all things. I believe He can work through us in unimaginable ways... and does. But I don't believe he violates our will... He allows us to feel the consequences of it. He is there to walk with us through it, and help us, if we are willing, to learn and grow in it...

"And this is where you may not believe me, or be able to believe me, or feel this is a cop-out—I don't know. But I have asked and sought for Him to help me cross this bridge—this gap—and at the end of the day, I am still here, on this side. And I don't feel I can cross it unless I make this choice now."

I remember looking at Chase as he paused at the part about the "bridge." A peace came over me that I couldn't explain in that moment, but what I could feel was his sincerity in trying to cross the bridge in his mind and heart toward reconciliation. Yet it felt like there was this invisible wall between us, a wall spiritual in nature. Somehow, God was allowing me to see it, and I was right there on the other side. Chase was so close. My heart silently called out to him.

Here I am, Chase! Right here. Just walk across the bridge! Try harder.

Then I heard my beloved husband say these words as he continued reading, and they burned into my consciousness.

"If this—choosing divorce—is the worst decision, the greatest mistake, I will ever make, then all I know is I still need to make it. I'm not making it in the hope that it is... I only know, or feel as deeply as I am capable of perceiving, that I need to make it. And the rest I have to trust the God I do know will use it to lead me to Him in love and compassion."

He finished the letter with a beautifully sincere, albeit maddening, affirmation of me.

"My choice of divorce is not about you, or a problem, or lacking, or anything else with you. It is about me and all of those things in me...

"Corrie, you have not simply been as faultless as any person is capable of being in all this; you have been as loving and giving and courageous as any person could be in this. In profound pain and hurt—undeserved and unjust—you have responded with love; with the love of God in you for me. And I have seen it, and known it, and have been changed by it...

"I will always be thankful for you. I will always admire you.

"I am sorry much of my part caused you pain... to be a source and reminder and cause of pain... and words will never hold how deeply I feel that...

"I love you, Corrie—and although you may not believe that for many reasons, and although I have failed to do so in all of the ways a husband should, it is true. And I hope someday you do, or will, know that."

Chase finished reading and looked at me with a weary yet sincerely caring gaze. Exhaustion began to settle into my bones as I stared back at him, so close to me yet light-years away.

Oh God, I gave everything. I put everything on the table. I don't understand this wall, and I don't know what to do with all this. But I know You do.

I realized my hands had been clenched since the start of the session, and I slowly softened my grip.

I trust You to keep leading me.

CHAPTER 20

Natasha Bedingfield

I remember exactly where I was when I heard it. In late spring of 2012, I was standing by the tall free-standing air conditioning unit in my apartment, trying to pray, when a simple and only slightly familiar name popped into my mind.

Natasha Bedingfield.

Huh? Natasha who? Hm… I think she is a singer.

I heard it again, clearly in my mind.

Natasha Bedingfield.

Why would I be thinking that on my own? Um… Okay. I think this is You, God.

Curious, I walked over to my computer and googled "Natasha Bedingfield—most recent album." Two clicks later, I arrived on a page with the lyrics to what appeared to be her most recent hit song, "Strip Me."

I noticed the song was thankfully not about literal stripping but instead about being stripped figuratively, just like I was experiencing in my life. She asked what you would find if you stripped everything else away from her. Even fully stripped of everything, she would be okay... because she would still have her voice. It might only be one voice in a massive sea of others, but it was her voice and could *not* be taken away.

Okay, God. You have my attention.

I kept reading. She compared her heart to a loudspeaker, always "on eleven."

That's when my jaw dropped. I read it out loud. "On eleven"? You're kidding me. My number with God, a reminder of His presence, his acceptance over me right where I was, and His perfect sense of timing.

Here it was in the song lyrics, jumping off the page at me. I had never heard that expression before.

I didn't have access to YouTube or iTunes at the time, so I couldn't download the song. Instead, I just made a mental note to try to find it or get a friend to download it for me.

After a couple of weeks, I was walking past a DVD shop by my apartment that I hadn't been to in over a year. Today, as I walked past it, the idea suddenly struck me.

Go inside.

But God, they are definitely not going to have Natasha Bedingfield.

If memory served, they only had one shelf of music CDs.

Go inside.

By this point in my pain journey, I knew I couldn't ignore an idea I sensed was from God. So I stepped into the once familiar shop, wall to wall with DVDs. I walked over to the tiny CD section and scanned the thirty or so discs on display by the checkout counter. I sighed as I noticed, of course, only the most famous names—Mariah Carey, Justin Bieber, Whitney Houston, Frank Sinatra, and the like. Not surprising in China.

So I left the store and kept walking but felt the idea persist.

Go inside.

I already had! So, why couldn't I let it go?

Okay, God. This is crazy, but I'll go back and try again. Why not?

This time, I called the store attendant over. She was carrying the iPad she used to check her stock. I spoke slowly so she could enter the name in English.

"Nimen zheli you meiyou Na-ta-sha Be-ding-...?"
("Do you have a CD by Na-ta-sha Be-ding-...?")

That's when I saw it, right at that moment. The *Strip Me* album, partially out of view under a stack of other CDs on the middle shelf! I pulled it out in disbelief and asked if it was new. She furrowed her brow and checked her digital catalog, and then replied in Chinese.

"Strange. I've never seen this CD before. It must be new. Only one of its kind. You want to buy it?"

I smiled. "Yes! I'll take it."

As I listened to *Strip Me* that night, the powerful beat and melody filled my senses. I felt the fight in me rise up—the fight against the voices of fear and rejection that weighed me down day in and day out. I was reminded that though we battle, God's love wins. Of course. It has already won.

God, You are so in this song.

I stood up and walked around my living room as I played it again.

This time, thoughts about my *Purple Phoenix Journey* blog started formulating. I was in the midst of designing a website to publish it.

But what, God? What would it be? How would it be focused? I need You to focus me. It could take so many directions.

The music kept flowing.

Then, in an instant, it was so clear.

A slogan. A focus. Three words.

Stripped.

That was the first word. Natasha sang louder, and I paced my living room, feeling alive and free and excited.

Another word flashed to mind.

Surrendered.

Yes! Exactly! I knew it was from Him. This was my journey.

Stripped. Surrendered…

The last word felt like it crashed on top of my head. I laughed out loud, tears of amazement welling up.

Soaring.

Of course, God! The perfect summary of what You're doing in the midst of my pain. You're allowing me to be stripped of what I thought I needed, bringing me to a place of surrender, and then letting me soar in Your freedom, soar over this storm.

The song finally ended, and I flopped down onto the cream-colored couch, eyes wide and glowing.

How fun. How brilliant! Exactly the sense of focus I had been crying out for.

"Strip Me" became my fight song, a way to fiercely declare I was valuable to the God of the Universe. I was loved, and my voice mattered to Him. With Natasha's epic voice blasting through my earphones, I would rage against my fears and dance like a wild woman on my treadmill, singing out in the faith room at the top of my lungs. Sorry, neighbors on the fourteenth and twelfth floors!

The Lord your God is in your midst, a mighty one who will save; he will rejoice over you with gladness; he will quiet you by his love; he will exult over you with loud singing.
—Zephaniah 3:17[1]

I reveled in this verse and the image I had of God continuously singing over us and over the earth like radio waves—His heart for people, His piercing love, His sheer joy over all of us, His confidence in His redemptive work and plan, and His power that has conquered all darkness.

When she wrote her song, I wonder if Natasha was tapping into that divine frequency. Her melodies and lyrics felt so inspired—bringing freedom, joy, and healing. God used her songs as such an amazing medium to speak to me.

I pondered what Natasha meant by the lyric comparing her heart to a loudspeaker. I wanted my heart to be a loudspeaker "on eleven" too—amplifying God's voice to the world by sharing pieces of His beauty, His hope, His song, and reminders of His perfect "11-11" timing.

In my pain, I was hearing His voice, even His song, over me. My heart was exploding to help others experience the same.

CHAPTER 21

A Rap and a Burning Bush

Click. Clack. Click. Clack.

The bike behind me is broken, I thought.
That's kind of annoying.

Click. Clack. Click. Clack.

I was biking home from my cardio kickboxing workout, which had consisted of seventy other Chinese women and me—sweat flying and vitality coursing through me as I locked in my focus and stayed in sync with the room pulsing with music. The last song of the night for our stretching time had been "Stand by Me," the same song I sang in the jazz club just a few months back.

God, thank You for that encouragement. You know I needed it.

By the spring of 2012, these types of conversations and experiences with God were almost a daily occurrence—my "11-11 moments." Sometimes He would grab my attention through street signs, license plates, or everyday objects.

Whatever it was, He was so good at interrupting my pain and helping me soar above it by keeping me focused on the spiritual realm.

I could feel my autonomy growing along with my confidence in my relationship with God, but my future was still so uncertain that I hung on His every word. Chase had followed through and started the divorce process, despite my fervent plea for reconciliation.

I got to the long stretch of city road to my apartment and started pedaling at a slow and steady pace under the raised highway. With each pedaling motion, the familiar pain about Chase began to rise to the surface. It would always hit me in waves when I was alone, especially on my bike. Even though the pain was not as intense as the first year, it was always there, right under the surface. Tears flowed as I thought of my absent husband, my best friend.

How could this be happening? Lord, I'm hurting.

Then, all of a sudden, it was quiet in my mind. I breathed out a sigh of relief for the stillness, feeling seen and loved.

Thank You for being here with me.

My thoughts felt slower as they came in one by one. I ran through my to-do list with God, item by item. Then it hit me—my college friend Kerri's wedding was coming up soon in May. My heart jumped.

Oh gosh! I haven't started preparing yet. Lord, You know I want to do something special for her.

Then I felt it again—seen, like He knew I was having that thought. He was with me in it, and I sensed it had come to mind for a reason. The road was quiet too, except for that annoying broken bike still behind me.

Click. Clack. Click. Clack.

I found myself listening to the sound again, noticing the rhythm it made. I smiled, strangely—an unexpected bit of amusement dropping into the annoyance, like a drop of blue food coloring into a bowl of water and quickly spreading. Then it dawned on me.

A rhythm… A rap. That's it!

Lyrics and a catchy melody started flooding my thoughts, clear as day. Thirty seconds later, I had the entire chorus and the start of the first verse. It was the story of Kerri and her fiancé. I started singing the chorus under my breath.

Her name is Kerri… She's gonna get married.
Her name is Kerri… She's gonna get married.

Laughter burst out of me. I was a suburban white girl who did not grow up listening to any rap music. I had never rapped in my life. I laughed the rest of the way home as the hilariously entertaining picture formed in my mind of the six of us—Kerri's closest college girlfriends—doing a rap together at her rehearsal dinner.

A rap to roast Kerri! God, that is hilarious and genius!

Click. Clack. Click. Clack.

The sound faded as the Chinese man finally passed me when I parked my bike at my apartment compound. I noticed the loose bike lock chain hanging down and hitting the side of his bike. He didn't seem to mind. I no longer did either.

A month later, in the US, I will never forget the utterly shocked—and maybe slightly terrified—look on Kerri's face when, during her very formal rehearsal dinner, the six of us girls burst out of the back room with microphones, singing and rapping.

A friend of mine on the worship team helped me lay down an instrumental beat track for the background, which helped me get the whole room clapping and moving. Everyone had erupted in thunderous laughter, and it was all we could do not to join in as we tried to keep up with the silly, fast-paced lyrics.

This was me being the true me! And though it was so strange and sad to be at the wedding without Chase—who all the girls knew and loved—I had a blast dancing and feeling free to be my bold and creative self.

Thank You, Lord, for inspiring me and giving me this experience of pure joy in the middle of my pain.

A few weeks after my return to Shanghai, I had another extraordinary experience with God. This time, instead of biking, I was walking down the sidewalk of the residential street next to my office. This was my much-needed work break, and as I walked and let my mind drift away from work, the familiar pain would surface. My lungs tightened and throbbed with uncertainty.

Step, step, step. My pace slowed as each step felt heavier than the last.

Why, God? How could this be happening? It hurts, God. It hurts so bad. I'm so scared. Where are You? I need You to speak to me.

Then, a stillness.

Corrie, I'm here. I'm all around you.

I felt the deep, sudden quiet of His presence. My lungs relaxed—breathing in peace, breathing out peace.

So glad You're here with me.

Step, step, step. Suddenly, a playful enjoyment was in each one, and I found myself giggling as my childlike voice came out.

You're really here.

Yes.

You're speaking.

Yes.

I'm seeing it. Feeling it. You're speaking through everything. All the time.

Yes.

Midstep, my eyes naturally fell on a bush by the sidewalk. A rounded wad of crumpled newspaper sat on top of it, grabbing my attention. Someone must have been aiming for the trashcan and missed, except there was no nearby trashcan. I stared at the crumpled wad and felt like it was somehow inviting me to pick it up.

God, You're funny. Why would I notice that? Should I really pick it up?

Sure.

Gross!

It was one thing to follow the crazy idea to sing in a clean— well, mostly clean—jazz club, but it felt insane for me to pick up a dirty piece of trash. Being clean was very important to me! Still, I couldn't shake the idea.

So, with a huge sigh, I turned aside like Moses to investigate this not-so-burning bush and reached over to grab the newspaper wad. While I was figuring out which two fingernails to grab it with, the last two Chinese characters on a line of crumpled text seemed to stare back up at me. I only knew the first one—"*tian* 天", meaning sky or heaven. I had no clue what the second one meant.

Okay, God, what do You have for me in "tian…"?

I heard nothing, but I knew He was there.

The three-minute walk back to my office was uneventful, heightened only by my twinge of curiosity for what these two characters meant. An online dictionary helped me determine the second character was "*lai* 籁" and that *tian lai* was an ancient musical flute and referred to nature sounds.

Hmmm…. Okay. That's cool, I guess.

But not that cool. It didn't really move me.

Oh well, God. Thanks for my moments of peace with You just now, anyway. But… I did sense You were right there with me when I picked up that newspaper, so… are You going to, like, have a Chinese guy playing an ancient musical flute come up to me on the street later or something?

I giggled.

That would be cool. Well, I'll just wait and see what You might do. I know You're here, and I know You know exactly what I'm thinking and what I need, so I'll just trust You have something in mind.

I almost forgot about that crumpled piece of newspaper. At almost midnight, as I was saying good night to my Chinese friend, Jolynn, who was staying overnight at my house, I suddenly remembered.

"Hey, Jolynn, what do the words 'tian lai' mean to you?"

"What?" she asked.

"*Tian lai*, the Chinese word."

"Oh, Corrie, who said that to you?" A smile lit up her face.

My curiosity piqued.

"Long story," I replied. "Can you just tell me what you think it means?"

My heart started beating faster.

"Well, obviously someone told you that about your voice, right? Your singing. Corrie, that's the highest compliment someone can give a singer. It means your voice is pure, open, and heavenly... So who said that to you?"

I sat there, stunned, my eyes glistening with tears.

"God," I said.

I showed her the newspaper, which I had brought home. The words were used as part of a car advertisement. She shook her head and smiled.

"Like I said, Corrie. That's the highest compliment someone could give a singer."

As she closed her bedroom door, I sat there with God on the couch and shared a moment of joy with Him—my Father, my guardian, my best friend. In the midst of crying out my pain about Chase, He had decided not to talk to me about him or how to move forward.

Instead, He cut to the core of me, and only He knew how to do it. Singing. Expressing my longings. Truth. Music. His heart. My heart. Beating together.

I'm not rejected, God. I'm not alone. I'm known, loved, and adored.

I don't think there is anything inherently special in objects or signs in and of themselves. We really don't have to go around hunting for "things."

What *is* special, though, are the moments during which we become aware of how surrounded we are by the indescribably powerful, supernatural, and calming presence of God. During the pure delight of these moments, I find He sometimes highlights to us certain objects that happen to be around us. If we only stopped and listened.

I think of them as tangible exclamation points to what He is already doing in the kingdom here in our midst, though not yet fully—this intermingling of the natural with the supernatural.

Tian lai.

I delighted in how quickly my painful moment had become a soaring one.

CHAPTER 22

The Year of Corrie—Part 2

"How are dreams two and three coming for 'The Year of Corrie'?" my coach, Lynette, asked during one of our calls in June of 2012.

"They are both happening back-to-back this summer!" I told her. "I'm still in shock it's all coming together."

I thought back to the end of last year when I had shared with her my two dreams of shaking Graham Cooke's hand and of organizing an eighth-grade reunion. Both dreams had felt as crazy and random as the scuba diving dream, but I had sensed a similar "Yes" in my spirit about them at the end of the call with Lynette that day. I decided to tackle them one at a time.

Graham Cooke, a renowned speaker and author, had been a tremendously positive influence in my life for over a decade.

How could it possibly work for me to meet him, God? Will he be here in China on a speaking tour?

I remember looking online at his tour schedule. There were no China dates, but I was shocked to notice he had an upcoming summer conference booked in Colorado in August! The dates of the conference were set for the exact same week I was already planning to be in Colorado for a family reunion—the only time that would work for me during my upcoming summer visit home to the US!

Peace had flooded my senses as I made arrangements to leave my family reunion early in order to attend one day of Graham's three-day conference.

Okay, now what about the eighth-grade reunion dream, God?

I looked at my packed schedule for the week in Colorado. I was set to arrive in Denver on Friday night, have a rest day on Saturday, and then head to the family reunion on Sunday.

Oh gosh, the eighth-grade reunion would have to be Saturday night.

That was the only day—a crazy twenty-four-hour window to potentially make it happen. I searched online and found a flight from Denver to Virginia departing at 9:00 a.m. Saturday morning and returning the next morning.

That's going to be very tight timing, but why the heck shouldn't I go for it? It's still "The Year of Corrie" after all!

At this point, I was on a roll. I called up the only two girls I was still in touch with from those years, Lara and Hannah, and they laughed with delight as I shared the idea with them.

"Let's do this!" they both exclaimed. The energy of that three-way call reminded me of the little girl excitement we always had, jumping around and playing together at one of our childhood sleepovers.

"I'll start searching for people on Facebook!" Lara exclaimed.

Hannah chimed in. "The school has a new campus now, but I'll call the old church campus to see if they'll let us walk through!"

We rolled up our sleeves and worked together throughout the spring to get the plan in place, roaring with laughter as we started going through old yearbooks. We reflected on our days playing Nerf football in the parking lot, making sure our plaid skirts "grazed our knees," and clapping the chalky dust out of black erasers behind the building.

Our hilarious invitation said in big letters "Do you see yourself pictured above?" with a collage of old photos of the thirty-five people who had shared those formative school years with us. Shockingly, we managed to find all of them on social media, and eleven people committed to attending. One person even planned to fly up from Florida!

Eleven. Of course, God.

When July finally came, I only had one part of my action-packed Colorado and Virginia trip left to plan—the overnight stay at the Denver airport before my morning flight to Virginia.

After searching online for over an hour, I found a few options for motels and sleeping lounges but just couldn't decide.

Why pay $150 for a few hours of sleep? Should I sleep in the airport?

In the current journey I was on with God—constantly listening to His voice and responding—I was normally more decisive and less prone to second-guessing myself. So that night caught me off guard.

God, help! Could You give me a sense of peace about where I should stay?

I heard nothing.

Where are You? Why are You being silent?

I sighed, scrolling through another full hour of hotel search engines and not feeling peace about any of the options. Frustrated, I gave up and went to bed, but as I lay there, an idea suddenly occurred to me.

What if I'm not feeling peace about booking a hotel, God, because You don't want me to book a hotel yet? Hm… Maybe You have something else for me that night in Denver?

Yes, I sensed in my spirit.

Stillness came over me, and I drifted off to sleep.

I started wondering what God might be up to as I took my flights a few days later—Shanghai to Los Angeles, then Los Angeles to Denver.

Would the nice family sitting next to me invite me to their house for a few hours? Would the flight attendant know of a secret lounge she would let me into with a couch to sleep on?

Nope.

Nice family next to me. Nice flight attendant.

No invitation. No secret free lounge.

Still no place to sleep.

Okay, God. I'm not seeing or hearing anything from You, but I know You know that...

Trust me.

My sense of anticipation remained, and after I grabbed my bags at the Denver airport, I began walking around the terminals. They were empty—like a ghost town. I looked at my watch. It was 2:00 a.m.

Where now, God?

As I rounded a corner, a mural painted on the wall suddenly caught my eye. It was a purple bird rising up from a fiery scene, reminding me of the name of my blog—*Purple Phoenix Journey.*

That's interesting. Am I on the right track? Hm… Okay, God, You're in this. But what are You up to? Should I just sleep in the airport? I could, but I'd really like to shower before my flight to Virginia tomorrow.

Ahead of me, I noticed a board with a courtesy phone and a list of nearby hotels. I decided to just move forward and call one, bite the bullet, and pay a high rate. Oh well. Maybe God had just wanted me to see that cool mural and practice trusting Him. Maybe I was just delusional and should have booked my hotel earlier and been more decisive. I didn't know.

All I knew was that despite feeling oddly at peace with my predicament, I was too tired to think anymore. I started calling hotels from the courtesy phone: No answer. Fully booked. Fully booked. No answer. One with a room but for $139.

Eek! I don't want to pay that much for just a few hours, but should I?

My mind churned with indecisiveness yet again.

God, come on! Are You really going to have me sleep on the floor in here?

"Hello, this is Aaron."

It was the next hotel on the list—the Comfort Inn. Aaron had a friendly voice, and I asked if he had a room for the night.

"Yes, I do have some availability."

"Great," I replied.

"Wait, so you're at the airport right now?"

"Yes," I said, curious.

"Oh, great, would you mind helping me out and just looking to see if there are any customer service people around? I have a... situation here, and I'm trying to get a hold of someone at the airport." He sounded relieved and anxious at the same time.

"Sure," I replied. Then, by frugal instinct, I added with a smile, "Then you'll give me a good rate, right?"

"How about $65.99?" he said cheerfully.

"Sure!" I replied and proceeded to run around the airport looking for a service person. Empty. Everyone had gone home. I called back and told him.

"Thanks for trying," he said.

I hopped in the airport shuttle and arrived thirty minutes later at the Comfort Inn hotel. It was close to 3:00 a.m.

Oh well, God. Thanks for at least giving me a good rate here at the last minute. Maybe You still have something up Your sleeve. Whatever it is, I'm open.

As I walked in the sliding glass doors with my luggage, a woman was pacing back and forth across the lobby. Her furrowed brow softened when she saw me.

"You're the one who was at the airport trying to help me, right? Thank you for trying!"

I stared at her blankly, noticing her disheveled appearance and weary eyes. Suddenly, I remembered Aaron's odd request.

"Oh! It was for *you*," I said. "Sorry I couldn't find an agent for you. Is everything okay?"

She shook her head. "Well, my connection flight in Denver was canceled, so the airlines gave me a Comfort Inn hotel voucher, but my taxi brought me here, which is the wrong Comfort Inn. Then he wouldn't come back to bring me to the right one, and I can't afford to order a new taxi. My new flight isn't until tomorrow at noon, and I've been on the phone with the airline management for over an hour."

I could tell she was at her wits end, and as I processed the situation, I felt the familiar warmth of inner stillness come over me.

Okay, God. There You are.

"So sorry to hear that," I said as I spied a young desk clerk waving me over to check in.

"It's okay," she said. "Hopefully the airlines can figure something out soon."

I walked over to the desk.

"Aaron, I presume?"

"That's me." He smiled.

I replied in a hushed tone. "I have an idea for that lady, and I wonder if you could help me with it. Would it be possible to change my king room to a room with two queens?"

He smiled again, eyes twinkling. "I have a better idea, since you're doing a good deed."

"Really?" I asked.

He clicked around on his computer and then handed me two keys.

"I'm giving you a free upgrade to a suite with two private queen rooms connected by a shared bathroom. How does that sound?"

"Perfect," I said, blinking back a tear.

There You are, God.

I walked over to the woman, who was still pacing the lobby with a phone pressed to her ear.

"You can end the call if you'd like to," I told her. "I just talked to Aaron, who gave me a double-room suite—plenty of room for you to share the space with me tonight."

Her eyes widened. "Are you serious? Oh my goodness, that would be incredible. You are too kind. I've never been this exhausted!"

"Happy to help," I said. "I'm Corrie, by the way."

"Robyn," she said.

"Nice to meet you, roomie!" I chuckled as we headed to the elevator, recognizing God's simultaneous answer to this woman's prayer and mine.

Wow, God. Why would I ever want my old mindset back where I was always trying to be in control all the time and never really expecting to hear from You? I was so tuned out to Your involvement in my daily life.

It became increasingly evident my role was listen, follow, and trust—even during moments of just hearing silence or the dreaded word "wait." I was to enjoy God's presence every moment, trusting His responses to my questions and prayers would come in His timing, not mine.

I felt like I was in training—learning to take risks, whether or not I always got it right. My summer adventure had just begun.

When I arrived in Virginia the next day, Hannah picked me up from Dulles airport, and we headed straight for her parents' house, where I would be staying that night. Just as we pulled into the long familiar driveway, Lara ran out to meet us. I threw my arms around both of them.

"I still can't believe this is happening. Thank you, ladies!" I squeaked with excitement.

"Corrie, how do you look so refreshed after your string of flights from China?" Lara asked.

"Well, I ended up getting an unexpected few hours of sleep last night and a shower this morning."

"Nice!" Hannah exclaimed. "But you'll have to tell us about that later because we gotta go if we're going to make it in time!"

I had not been back to the church since eighth grade. We arrived and stared up at the two-story red-brick building. Nothing had changed.

As we set up in the fellowship hall, I shook my head.

"I can't believe they just let us be in here and didn't charge us. This is the perfect place for the reunion. I can't wait to see everyone!"

We arranged for all eleven people to sit in a circle for the slide show and other activities we had planned before the walking tour. I stared at the thirty-year-old faces I hadn't seen in sixteen years.

"You guys, I feel like we're all a bunch of cousins who just haven't seen each other in a while. Does anyone else feel like that?"

They laughed and nodded.

The next few hours were pure joy. I had designed a game called "You just might be a former student here if...." Everyone filled in the blank with things like "... rainy days give you the urge to play silent speedball" and other inside jokes we all understood. We rolled with laughter.

The group was also small enough to have a meaningful time of round-robin sharing, answering questions from a list we had prepared about teachers who impacted our lives, or a significant highlight, or challenge in recent years.

When it was my turn, I sang my eighth-grade presidential campaign song word for word to a roaring applause. Then I opened up about my current and pending divorce. Saying Chase's name seemed out of place in my childhood world where no one knew him, a world that only knew me as me. Here, I was just Corrie—a leader, friend, and organized project manager who was fun and creative.

I was someone before Chase, and I'm someone without him.

This thought had become more familiar to me over the past year but was now beginning to really take root.

The reunion proved to be an important touchpoint not only for me but for everyone who came. As I flew back to Denver the next day, I was physically exhausted but totally refreshed in my spirit.

The Colorado gathering with dozens of extended family members filled me with even more warmth and life. Then, as planned, I left a day early to drive to nearby Castle Rock, where the massive sky and open landscape invited me to lift my gaze to the heavens.

The Graham Cooke conference was in a large church, and I found an empty seat on the aisle close to the front of the sanctuary. When he walked onto the stage, I smiled as I first noticed his feet. He was not wearing shoes, just purple socks.

What a cool, quirky guy! I thought, never having seen him before.

He was a bit older, maybe early sixties, with gray wisps of hair on his head that matched his short goatee. His shoulders had a slight forward hunch as he peered out over the large auditorium, and he adjusted his navy shirt over a slightly rounded belly. His British voice was immediately familiar from all the talks I'd listened to over the years.

"If it's not too good to be true, then it's not God," he said.

I breathed deeply as the scriptures he read over us from his well-worn Bible began to soak in and as he told story after story about the God of the impossible. I was a beloved child, a beloved daughter, a warrior, and a friend of God.

During our first coffee break, I saw my chance and made a beeline for Graham, hand outstretched.

"I'm Corrie," I said as he squeezed my hand.

"Nice to meet you, Corrie," he replied, his fatherly eyes wrinkling at the corners.

"You have no idea how thrilled I am to meet you, Graham. God opened up a way for me to make it over here from China, and I'm truly honored."

My trip ended with a long drive under turtle-shaped clouds painted in hues of gold and purple in a brilliant sunset sky. I was feeling inundated with signs of love from God, subtle reminders He was around and I was okay. His plan and love were bigger than the pain I was experiencing and the endless questions swirling in my mind about my absent husband.

How strange to have planned and experienced this trip entirely on my own without Chase. Our lives felt so separate now, and while I still hoped for reconciliation, I surrendered the outcome of our marriage more and more. My focus was exactly where it needed to be, and I was having a blast.

Dreams number two and three for "The Year of Corrie"—*check*!

Thank You, Lord.

CHAPTER 23

Walking in Delight

I wrote this poem in 2012 as I reflected on the stillness and closeness with God I was experiencing, especially during my "11-11 moments."

Walking in delight
Every action, every deed
Every thought
Slower speed
"Halt," I say
The race is off
The rules are a lie
The referees scoff
I'm in a place
Slowing my pace
Gazing around
Pleasant the sound
Of each little thought

Savoring sweet
Oppression has ended
I hear a new beat
It's Your heart, it's Your song
I can now sing along
It's a dance, it's a gander
Delightful meander
Erasing my past and my whole list of tasks
I can see, I can see!
I can finally be me
Not controlled, not contrived
Just a freedom to thrive
And relax in my breathing
The enemy seething...
With no place to land on me
No place to stand on me
What shall I do now?
Things here are so light
Why was life just to-dos, and each day a big fight?
I want life on Your terms, God
To walk in delight

CHAPTER 24

Fibers in a Tapestry

I remember one not so special day, I was finishing up work at the upper school campus. Our admissions office there sat just inside the front gate of the school with three large windows. We called it "the fishbowl." During the day, the campus buzzed with teenaged students in navy-blue uniforms, scurrying between classes and then racing to sports practice.

By now, it was dark out and gloomy but still quite warm for early fall. At least an hour had passed since the last soccer whistle. I locked my laptop into my desk drawer and emerged from the fishbowl into the outdoor gloom, blinking in surprise as a few wet drops pelted my face.

That morning, I had decided to ride my bike to work. I reached behind me to find an empty pocket where my purple rain poncho normally was. I sighed. It was going to be a cold, wet fifteen-minute ride home, so I hustled toward the covered staff parking lot where I often parked my bike or scooter among the dozens of others.

I bent down to unlock the chain and then grasped the handlebars to roll my bike back. It wouldn't budge. The front wheel was stuck and refusing to turn. *What? How strange.* A heavy scooter must have hit the front when passing by and jammed the gears. *Great, this is all I need after my scooter was stolen last week.*

Okay, Lord, I guess I'm catching a taxi home.

I shuffled slowly out the main gate and off campus, rain splattering on my umbrella and on parked cars lining the street for parents' night.

Then I heard it. A tiny cry. Then another one.

Meow. Meoooowww!

The pitiful meowing grew louder, comically mirroring my transportation woes. I was intrigued. Then something occurred to me: If my bike hadn't been stuck, I would have raced by and never heard the cry at all. Familiar now with God's unexpected promptings, I paused.

God, are You setting me up to rescue a kitty?

The idea immediately resonated with me.

That would be so cool! So... intimate and thoughtful of You.

A little, warm someone to greet me when I came home at night, cuddle with me on the couch, and remind me of rest and stillness as only a cat can do.

I knelt down by a parked SUV, and sure enough, I spied a little gray kitten crouching on top of its front tire, eyes wild and legs shaking. So cute! I reached out, but it flinched back and scurried further under the vehicle.

I couldn't shake the feeling God had caused me to notice this little cat, so I made another attempt, to no avail.

Okay, God, if this is from You, could You have him walk out and cuddle into my arms in the next ten seconds? That's really all I have before I have to go.

I counted slowly... eight... nine... ten. No sound, no kitten movement.

I decided to continue on my way but then felt nudged to turn around. Maybe I hadn't tried hard enough.

I ran back to my office and grabbed a sturdy canvas bag, and then came out and crouched down again, making kissing noises to coax the kitten out. When he finally moved his little body to the front of the tire, I reached out my hand slowly to let him sniff me as I gently encircled my fingers around his tiny body.

I smiled. Almost there! I pulled my hand toward the bag, but the kitten had dug its nails into the tire and was clinging to it with all its might. A tug-of-war.

Finally, he released his grip, and I seized the moment, lifting him up and over into the bag. His head jerked up and eyes went wild as he frantically scratched around the bag, writhing his body around inside it. Before I could react, he had leaped up and scrambled out... right back under the car.

My heart was pounding.

Okay, God! I tried! But why did You show me this cat if You didn't want me to save it?

I stared down the dark street, hearing only the drumbeat of the steady rain and the distant honking of taxis.

Well, I know You know what I'm thinking, and You're definitely up to something. I suppose You could still have the kitten show up at my office tomorrow... or something. I'll just leave this with You. I've done everything I feel I can, and more, and now I'm late to dinner with Leanna.

I flagged down a taxi with a twinge of disappointment but also with the thought that if God were really to bring a cat into my life, it would have to be a perfect, well-behaved one. I had no emotional capacity to deal with a wild and jumpy street cat.

A few minutes later, Leanna was ladling James's delicious homemade stew into my bowl, and I shared the experience with her. She smiled wistfully.

"Oh, Corrie, it would have been so nice to have been given a little kitty from God! It would be so like Him to give you one!"

"I know! That's why I tried so hard."

The next morning, my eyes darted around the street as I approached my office. No kitten. No meowing.

I sighed.

Oh well. God, You see the bigger picture.

A week went by, and thoughts of the scared kitten had faded. Friday night arrived, and I was at Jeena's house for a girls' night along with another friend, Angela. When I say "house," I mean "apartment," because most of the population in Shanghai lives in high-rise apartment buildings. Jeena's was an old traditional *"shi ku men"* apartment (one with a courtyard)—a fifth-floor walkup with dark, creaky wood floors, high ceilings, and massive windows overlooking the downtown area just next to the famous Bund skyline strip.

Jeena was a new friend from church but someone who immediately felt like an old friend—often the case with people in the expat faith community. Several months prior, we had been sitting opposite each other in a charming little vegetarian hot pot restaurant in the French district. My entire two-year crisis and faith story had unexpectedly tumbled out, and she just got it immediately.

"Corrie, what you're walking through is beyond devastating, yet you have this joy. Clearly, the Lord is guiding you on an adventure with Him. It's so exciting! What is He going to do next? I want to know everything!"

Jeena became an instant cheerleader for this new journey of faith I was on, and she was always chiming in with her own experiences of hearing from God as well. She was American and full of joyful energy, like water to my soul after wandering around in what felt like a desert, trying to make sense of my pain with Chase.

For our girls' night, the three of us ordered in Sichuan Chinese food from a local place, baked cookies together, and shared stories for hours about what God was doing in our lives. The night stretched to 1:00 a.m., and Angela and I finally stood up to head out.

"Want to share a taxi?" she asked.

"Sure."

We made our way down the five sets of dark stairs and emerged onto the deserted street. I was struck by the quietness there. Shops must close early in that part of the city. The buildings were a century-old and washed gray in the moonlight. Their grand stern faces were softened only by occasional arched doorways with ornate embellishments. The streetlights illuminated a few scattered bottles and plastic bags.

"It's actually such a beautiful night. You want to walk for a bit?" I asked.

She nodded. Pleasantly cool evenings only happened two months of the year in Shanghai.

We picked the least smelly direction and started walking. My eyes wandered up to an old building on my right, a glint of gold from a symbol on it catching my eye: a golden eagle with two snakes. I paused to pull out my phone and snap a photo of it as well as the Chinese characters next to it so I could look them up later.

Angela, who had stopped beside me, suddenly made a little squeak as she and I both noticed a little black and white street kitten padding over toward us. It made a calm little route around both of our ankles and blinked up at us expectantly.

That's when it hit me. I laughed and looked around. Deserted street.

Really, God? Actually, of course.

I reached down and gently, easily, lifted up the little precious creature into my arms. It immediately settled comfortably and started purring. Not a flinch, not even a twitch. Angela laughed and gave me a quizzical look.

"I think I'm going to take him. I'll explain it on the way." I couldn't stop smiling.

The gentle purring continued against my right arm as I hailed a passing cab with my left. Our eyes were glued to our black and white bundle as I shared with Angela about the previous week's tug-of-war with the gray kitten by my office.

"I honestly think God was preparing me to receive this," I mused. "I would have never thought to get a cat for myself. I'm way too much of a neat freak for that. Yet, somehow, this makes sense. I've just never had one though. Have you?"

She nodded.

"I grew up with them my whole life. I can come over right now and help you get set up if you want."

"Oh, yes! That would be amazing."

By the time we pulled the kitten out of the bathtub at my apartment, it was close to 2:30 a.m. I placed him into a big cardboard box with towels and a water bowl. Angela was in her element.

"Okay, this should work for tonight. Tomorrow morning, you can get a litter box and set it up right here. He'll catch on really quickly. And there's a vet close by where you can get his shots. You're going to do great."

I hugged her as she left. "I can't even tell you…"

"This was such a setup," she said. "I loved every minute."

In amazement, I collapsed onto my cream-colored couch. That night, I had felt energized, full of life. Not late to a dinner, not fighting the rain. That night, I "happened" to be with Angela, a cat expert. I sat quietly for a while to process it. I didn't even have to try earlier. Nothing had felt forced; no tug-of-war, no pleading. I had just opened my eyes and ears, ready to respond and receive.

Little kitten eyes blinked up at me from the box. His black and white fur was still damp, and I lifted him up to cradle him in the nook of my elbow. The intoxicating purring started again, as if on cue.

But what is your name, little one?

The next day, my Chinese colleagues peered at my phone as I held up the photo I had snapped of the old building where the new kitten had found me.

"Oh!" they said, instantly recognizing it and reading the Chinese characters. "That is an old government building, a lab center for the analysis of fabric fibers. It's the place they examine fibers under microscopes to determine if they are authentic."

I just stood there and took it in, connecting with the word "fiber," which had stood out to me. In my walk with God, I felt like a fiber being examined and extracted of everything inauthentic.

I love it! His name is Fiber.

"Fiber" also made me think of the fibers of a tapestry. Most days, all I saw was the chaotic reverse side of the tapestry, which was the crisis I was in. It was a mess so overwhelming I often found myself taking ten-minute walks around the neighborhood just to release the relentless ache, tears streaming down my face.

How could there be good in this, God? Bring Chase home, Lord. Make it right, God! Make it right. You have to make it right.

When I got home that night, I felt soothed by the gentleness of little Fiber nuzzling my elbow, padding his front paws back and forth against my forearm, like he was pressing two invisible buttons—left, right, left, right.

The scribbled words in my journal were smudged with tears as I wrote what I sensed God saying to me:

It is right, Corrie. It's beautiful. You can't see it yet. You will. It's so beautiful. You'll see. Just wait. Trust me.

You are becoming wholehearted, able to walk in abundance. I know the pattern. I use it all for good. All of it. Every part of it. None of the pain is wasted. None of it. You'll see. Every fiber. All these encounters with me. I'm weaving them. You're right where I want you to be. Fiber is a reminder for you. I know you. You're okay. Just rest.

Okay, God. Okay.

I took Fiber to the vet that night for his shots, and the vet's eyes widened as he examined him. He couldn't believe how healthy and friendly Fiber was after living on the streets.

"*Zhe shi feichang hanjian de,*" he said.

(That is very rare.)

Fiber became my little friend and roommate. I hadn't realized how much I'd missed talking to someone when I was home alone.

"I'm home, Fiber!"

"You look like you had a good day, mister."

"What is next on our list for today, Fiber?"

"You were hungry today, little guy, huh?"

"I'll be back soon!"

This simple daily chatter, along with the endless purring and warmth of my little cat, was a balm to my hurting soul. Fiber was always there—a comfort and a reminder to me that God was weaving the fibers of my pain and all my experiences into a massive, beautiful tapestry as I continued to walk in hope.

CHAPTER 25

Funeral in the Forest

Have a funeral for Chase.

What, God?

In mid-October, 2012, I was strolling in silence through a lush bamboo forest, feeling stillness in my spirit and listening for God. A friend and I were there on a trip exploring the mountains of Zhejiang, China. She was walking about fifty yards ahead while I took a slower pace and immersed myself in the natural beauty around me.

The towering bamboo trees soared around me, reaching two or three stories high. Feathery green leaves adorned their slender outstretched arms, bending toward me on the path. Only occasional rays of warm sunlight peeked through the abundant gray-green stalks, eager to light up any patch they could on the soft path before me.

Being away from the hustle of the city and the constant buzzing of technology was exactly what I needed. I hadn't received an email from Chase's lawyer in a while, but I still cringed every time I'd see Chase's or his lawyer's name in my inbox. Even though this limbo period was painful, I was glad the process was going slowly. I had even started praying the papers would get lost in the mail, which actually did happen with the delivery receipt of the summons and petition. Having only divorce-related correspondence with Chase since our final counseling session in February was so odd.

Have a funeral for Chase, I heard again, catching me totally off guard.

The voice was gentle and kind but also resolute, and my tears came in a rush like the waterfall I could see up ahead. I whispered back to God:

No. How could I? Say goodbye? What do You mean?

Like a funeral.
That time is over. That season is over.
Remember the good things, Corrie.
Remember what I did in that season.
Remember who he was to you in that season.
Remember the things I was to you through him in that season.
It was good, Corrie.
It was me.
I had so much good for you in that season. I want you to reflect on it.

But God, it's painful. It's so painful. I don't want to face all of that. I miss so many things about us. About You in us.

I know. I know.

God, I'm so tired. I'm tired of this tension, tired of this sadness, tired of this longing. So tired. I want to be free.

Corrie, you are.
Remember what I spoke to you, Corrie. Remember.
There is a higher calling, if you choose it.
There is a word. I released a vision. Do you believe it will be fulfilled?
That it is being fulfilled?
That I am the God of the impossible?
Remember.
Remember.

Memories from the two previous years of pain came in waves as I approached the surging waterfall. I remembered that first Christmas in crisis, 2010. I was praying with two friends in the US, and one of them had a vision of a calm place in the midst of a storm.

She had said, "Corrie, I sense God has a royal calling for you, in relationship with Him, in His kingdom. He is offering you a deep level of faith and intimacy with Him, a place where abundant resources are accessed and where His heart of love sets captives free. You don't have to choose it. It will be a painful journey that will require sacrifice. But there will also be great reward and deep intimacy with Him."

I remember responding, "Yes, I choose this." And I had kept choosing it, level after level of surrender, learning to be *content whatever the circumstances.*[1]

I breathed out: Whatever… the… circumstances.

Yes, this is a royal calling—being so aware of My presence that you focus your eyes up, not down and not in front of you. Every problem, every conflict, every ounce of pain is an opportunity for training.
Awake, awake, arise.
Step into the place of royalty, of strength, of victory in the battle. Problems are opportunities to experience Me.

I reflected back to 2011, walking through life reading a book Jody had given me called *Hinds' Feet on High Places*. It was an allegorical journey of a little deer named Much-Afraid, who was being led to high places, her journey mirroring my own in an uncanny way.

I remember getting to a passage in the book that caused the world around me to go quiet. The section was called "Detour through the Desert." In it, the Shepherd (the God character) talked about Abraham, Joseph, and many other followers of God who had walked the road of fiery trials.

> They came to learn the secret of royalty, and now you are here, Much-Afraid. You, too, are in the line of succession. It is a great privilege, and if you will, you also may learn the lesson of the furnace and of the great darkness just as surely as did those before you. Those who come down to the furnace go on their way afterward as royal men and women, princes and princesses of the Royal Line.[2]

Immediately, I prayed:

Yes, I choose this path, the path of listening to Your voice, God, walking by faith and not by sight for a purpose bigger than just me. I choose to be immersed in Your reality. To find my hope here. Not in a person. Not in an outcome. You restore me. You heal me. You equip me for this fight.

My shoulders straightened as I replayed in my mind what I had just heard a few minutes before in the bamboo forest.

Have a funeral for Chase.

I still didn't comprehend this, but I speculated God was preparing me for a renewed Chase to come home to me.

Okay, God. I will.

When I returned home to Shanghai, I made a funeral plan for Chase—a memorial to commemorate the Chase I had known.

I went home to search for something small I could burn as a symbolic gesture of closure, saying goodbye to the old Chase. I came across one last thing of his that remained in my apartment—a pair of socks.

Perfect.

I planned a trip to the countryside the following Friday, and my sweet Chinese friend Lily offered to come with me as a support since she lived out that way. I accepted and had brought along a book of matches and a little square cookie tin I had found in a cupboard.

When we arrived, I noticed the air faintly smelled of fertilizer and burning compost. The sun was setting over fields as she led me to a simple wooden bridge over a narrow creek. The evening was pleasantly cool, and not a soul was around. Lily sat there on the bridge with me in complete silence for what felt like a long while as I stared out into the distance, captivated by the fading light.

I remember the delicate pressure of her hand on my shoulder as my tears started to flow.

Okay, God. Here we go.

I lit the match and watched as the pair of socks began to glow and catch flame in the little gray tin.

Memories flooded in. As if I were giving a eulogy, I spoke out loud and sobbed as I expressed my gratitude to God for the gift of meeting Chase twelve years prior. I talked to the invisible audience about the lightheartedness Chase had brought into my little teenage life and the joy, fun, and laughter we had shared over the years. I shared moments of our incredible wedding and the excitement of setting up our first apartment.

I reveled in the days we had worshiped God together and learned about hearing His voice with our California church community. My heart soared as I reflected on our adventurous decision to move to China and the long hours in language school together. I shared about the meaningful connections we made with friends from all over the world and the many trips we had taken around China and Southeast Asia.

I thanked God for how Chase had encouraged me to step out of my comfort zone and become a manager at my job, for the fun we'd had in launching the study abroad program he now ran, and for the relationships we'd formed with the program's college students.

Such beauty we had experienced together, Chase and I. Two hours had gone by, and the final glowing sock ember had just gone dark.

I felt empty yet strangely full.

Goodbye, Chase.

I sensed I was not just saying goodbye to the former Chase but also goodbye to the prison of fear and condemning Noise that once filled my mind incessantly, as well as goodbye to my prior reliance on a husband to quiet those voices. I was stepping into my royal calling—my true and primary identity as a beloved daughter of God.

CHAPTER 26

Three Dreams

"Corrie, this is Ken. I'm sorry for calling so late."

In late October, I was surprised to see Chase's boss, dean of the university study abroad department, was calling from the US. I knew him well, but he had never called me directly. Ken's tone was serious as he went on.

"I didn't know if you knew this, but Chase just resigned from his position as director of our Shanghai program."

"No, I didn't, Ken. Thanks for letting me know. I haven't seen Chase in quite a few months. I know you're aware he started divorce proceedings back in February, and we're just in touch for procedural things at this point."

"It's still so hard to believe, Corrie. I'm so sorry."

"Me too," I replied, trying to process the news about Chase. Ken's voice was full of caring concern.

"Well, as you can imagine, with Chase as the founding director for the program, we are at a bit of a loss for what to do. He said he will stay another two months until the end of the semester in December, but we have another semester starting up in January with no director."

He paused.

"We have an idea, and it's a bit out there, but I wanted to mention it to you. I know you're happy in your role at the international school, but, Corrie, you're the only one who knows this study abroad program. We are wondering if there is any way you might be able to step in on an interim basis as director?"

My jaw dropped.

Chase's position.

"Ken, I'm honored you would think of me."

"We think the world of you, Corrie, and we know you'd do a great job as interim director. In fact, we'd love for you to consider applying for the long-term director position when we open the formal search in early spring. We just have this immediate need at the moment for someone to start in January."

I paused.

"I will need to give this some serious thought and prayer, Ken. I have no idea how I might be able to take a temporary leave of absence from my admissions role at the school, but who knows. Can I call you in a few days?"

"Of course," he said. "And please know we are praying for you, and for Chase, as you go through this difficult time."

"Thanks so much, Ken." I hung up the phone, my head spinning. I needed to call Leanna.

Ask me, I heard in that moment, so I stopped dialing and put the phone down.

Okay, God. I'll ask You first. What do You think of this?

Immediately, three dreams I'd recently had came rushing to the front of my mind. In one, I had walked into Chase's empty office and found a large duffle bag packed and sitting on the floor. Another was similar, but in this one, the computer was still on and there was a digital picture frame displaying visual photos, as if it were still his office and he had just stepped out for a bit. The final dream was of me walking down the road toward the study abroad facility with Chase, only to watch him turn and walk in the opposite direction while I continued on, alone.

I had written these down in my journal when they happened but hadn't thought much about them. I was often having vivid dreams at night that felt very random in the moment.

Wow, God. That's what those were about.

Yes.

I knew I had my answer, even if it meant resigning from my admissions position where I'd worked for over four years.

Unrelated to this, I had also strongly considered going to a three-month ministry training school in Mozambique sometime the following year and had been trying to discern the best time for raising it with my boss.

I decided to go for broke and ask my boss about both opportunities together. I was nervous yet determined the next day when I called her at our headquarters in Hong Kong.

"The interim director role would be January to July of next year," I told her. "Then the ministry school in Africa would be from August to October." I could hear my heart beating.

She hesitated.

"Corrie, I have to tell you, this is very unexpected. I will need to think about it."

"Absolutely. I really appreciate your consideration and understand this is a wildly unusual request. I would love to find a way to continue working here and will send you a potential plan I've put together for stabilizing my admissions team in my absence. If the best thing would be for me to resign, I understand that as well."

I'll never forget what my boss said when she called me the following day.

"Corrie, I was brushing my teeth this morning, and I had an idea."

"Really?" I laughed.

"What if you postpone the Africa trip to October, come back to our school for a couple of months after your first six months away, and get things in order with your team before you leave again?"

"I think that's definitely possible!" I said in shock. The ministry training programs in Mozambique ran all throughout the year.

"Good," she said. "Because we don't want you resigning, Corrie. You've done a great job building up the team, and as you suggested in your plan, we could promote Jana to the acting head of admissions role while you're away. It won't be easy at all, but I can step in when needed to support Jana, and we can do our best to make it work."

She paused, and I held my breath.

"Your leave will be unpaid, of course, but when you return full-time in January 2014, we actually have a promotion in mind for you to head of admissions for the entire China region. It would be a new role we would create for you."

"Oh, wow…" I stammered. She went on.

"As part of it, the school owns a two-bedroom apartment near your main campus office that is about to be vacant. It's a nice one that normally we give to a school principal and their spouse, but this particular one is on the smaller side and better for one person. We want to offer it to you starting in January."

"Oh my goodness, I'm so honored and grateful. I hardly know what to say." I was familiar with the apartments she was referring to. They were part of a luxurious complex with floor-to-ceiling marble lobbies, expansive gardens, a pool, and a fantastic view.

"Just promise me you'll come back," she said.

"I definitely plan on it," I replied. "I have no intention or desire to apply long term for the study abroad director role."

I hung up the phone, still in total shock and amazement. Nothing could have prepared me for this call.

God! A new house? A promotion after being gone for eight months next year? Oh my gosh! Such confirmation.

Ken was thrilled to receive my call that night.

"Whew! That's fabulous news, Corrie. We really need you, and the students will be so fortunate to have your help through the end of their academic year. I'll let Chase know so he can do handover stuff with you before he leaves. And we'll get a regular call for me and you moving forward as well."

The reality started to sink in. I would be stepping into Chase's position. The role was important and felt intimidating. Study abroad program directors I knew were almost twice my age, and I wasn't yet convinced I was as capable as Chase.

The more I reflected on it, though, the more it resonated this was a redemptive step God had set into motion to shift me away from the place I had dwelled for over a decade—in Chase' shadow as his adoring fan, known simply as "Chase's girlfriend" and later "Chase's wife." People believed in me to step up and take on his job!

I received it as a challenge and an opportunity to lean on God and exercise the new boldness I was feeling to function independently in my relationship with Him. I knew He would help me.

A month or so later, in December of 2012, I was waiting in my apartment for Chase, who was supposed to arrive any minute. He was coming to hand over the keys to the facility and the other required paperwork for the program. I felt nervous because I knew he wasn't thrilled I was taking his job, and also because I'd only seen him once since February.

I thought back to a day in August when I also had been waiting for Chase's knock at my door. Two things had happened while I waited. The first was seeing two birds land on my balcony on the thirteenth floor. Birds never stayed up there like that or came that high, but there they were, just peering into my apartment and hopping around for several minutes. The second thing that happened was an email that popped up from a friend from my former Bible study in the US who I hadn't talked to or seen in six years.

> Corrie, I cannot explain why, but I was just awakened with a strong feeling that God wanted me to reach out to you. It is 2:00 a.m. here, but I cannot get back to sleep, and every time I try, I see your face. Not sure what that means, but know that you have my prayers

and support right now. The verse on my heart right now is Jeremiah 29:11.
Love in Christ,
Alex

Those two experiences had been God's beautiful preparation for Chase arriving at my apartment on that summer day, the day he told me he was moving on and planning on dating other people. It had been a very painful conversation, but I had felt covered and prepared.

Remembering those two beautiful August gifts from God helped calm my breathing as Chase's knock sounded once again at my door. Now it was a cold day in December. Little did I know this would be my last real conversation with him.

CHAPTER 27

The Final Push

Seeing Chase walk into my (our) apartment and sit on the couch was both odd and familiar. We managed a bit of small talk for a few minutes. He told me about his new job, and then I started asking him some procedural handover questions about the study abroad program. What were the discipline issues with the students so far during the semester? Who were the resident advisors? And so on.

"Corrie, I honestly don't know why you're doing this. What are you planning on telling the students, that you're my wife?" he asked, a skeptical look on his face.

I caught his eye and felt surprisingly calm and unwavering as I replied.

"Chase, I'm doing this because I feel led to do it. I don't have any agenda to wreck the students' perception of you. When I introduce myself next month, I just plan to tell them that I'm your wife, since I am your wife, and that we've been separated for a while. That's all they need to know."

I paused, watching him shift in his seat.

"Corrie, I'm moving on. I told you that this summer. I know you're still waiting around for me to 'wake up' or something, but in reality, that is not going to happen."

"Chase, I respect you feel you need to move on. And I also respect my wedding vows. Until we are divorced, I am still your wife, and I need to do what I feel God is calling me to do, bottom line. I'm sorry you disagree, but I've made my decision about the position."

"Okay, I guess." He shrugged and handed me a few keys and some paperwork, shifting gears.

"There's something I want to tell you," he said. "A girl I've been dating since the summer... She's from Canada and teaches English in the city. It's become very serious between us, and we are planning to be together long term. In fact..."

He paused.

"She's pregnant."

I froze.

"With twins," he said. Again, like an actor in a play, he must be rehearsing his lines with me.

This news had nowhere to land. It just hovered in the air between us like a bizarre, unwelcomed bumble bee.

Twins. He had said it so matter-of-factly. I asked when they had found out.

"October," he said. "It was unexpected, but we're very happy."

Oh God.

"Is that the reason you resigned?" I asked.

"No. Honestly, I had just gotten the offer from my new job and resigned from my current job when we found out."

I stared down at my palms as he got up to leave.

"I just wanted to tell you in person," he said.

I remember walking him to the door and saying something like "If I were a different person, I might be tempted to say 'get the hell out of my house' or some other rude thing. But I'm not, so I'll just say bye for now."

As I closed the door behind him, I tried to think of something authentic I could actually say to him. I sensed this might be our last conversation, and I didn't want to end on that. Obviously, "congratulations" was not in the realm of possibility.

I thought about what had just happened. My *husband* had just told me his new girlfriend was having twins. My husband, who had wanted to be free from our marriage and do his own thing, would unexpectedly be changing diapers for the next three years. What an interesting scenario.

I wonder what You're going to be doing in him, God. I think he's going to learn a lot as a dad. I think it might humble him and ground him in some important ways.

There we go. That was it. I could say something like that. I dialed Chase's number. He'd only been gone a few minutes.

"Hey," he answered.

"Hey, I was thinking about it and wanted to tell you... I'm glad you're going to be a father. That's all."

He paused.

"Thanks. I appreciate that."

Soon after that day, during a prayer and worship meeting I was attending, I found myself writing a goodbye letter to Chase in my journal. It poured out on page after page, not to challenge him to step up and reconcile as I'd done before. This time, it was to say goodbye. It was not for him to ever read, but just for me to express my heart. As I wrote it, I felt another layer of closure happening inside me.

This was the first time I allowed myself to consider the idea that the closure the Lord had been bringing me through since the October "funeral" moment in the bamboo forest might not just be about our old marriage or the old Chase but might be a permanent closure.

But God, why for so long have You had me contend for the redemption of our marriage if it wasn't going to happen?

I wrestled with this question over the next few months as I stepped into Chase's old job, still full of faith God could do the impossible but getting more indicators of closure.

One came from my friend Don. He and Chase had been close friends who talked a lot during the first year of the crisis before Chase had more fully isolated himself from our friends. I remember Don and his wife coming up to me after small group one night.

"Corrie, not to be weird, but I had a dream about you last night. In the dream, I saw this huge open filing cabinet drawer, like twenty feet long, full of all these note cards with descriptions about things you've done as you've contended for your marriage with Chase."

"Okay," I said, fascinated.

"The notecards said great things like prayers you've prayed, ways you've trusted God, ways you've helped people, and ways you've loved Chase. But then the huge drawer suddenly closed, and my sense was it was over. The time was done."

"Wow, thanks so much for sharing that," I told him.

God, what is happening?

I could feel it. More and more, I was starting to envision a life without Chase, something previously unthinkable.

In my new role as interim director for the study abroad program, Chase's students were understanding and didn't ask many questions. They had their own lives and travels to think about, and I threw myself into the job during those months to give them an incredibly meaningful semester. It was strange and painful at first to be doing the role alone when Chase and I had always interacted with the students as a couple.

However, the pain was surpassed by the sense God was up to something redemptive in the midst of it. I felt that as I rearranged the furniture in Chase's office to make it my own, reorganized some things that had fallen through the cracks under his watch, and found a creative consequence for a couple of misbehaving students who turned things around by agreeing to organize a hugely successful basketball tournament for the whole group of thirty students.

Three other standout moments from that semester were giving a "Braveheart-style" speech to the students during our Tibet trip when half the group got altitude sickness and needed some inspiration to keep moving, being an audience member of the very first student variety show, and walking into my office on my birthday to discover the students had filled it with eight hundred balloons!

My confidence grew in leaps and bounds during those six months as I navigated challenges and established new systems for the program.

As the semester came to a close, I asked the students what they wanted to leave behind.

The Shanghai program tradition was that each student group would vote and leave their "mark" on the facility—a signed wooden bench in the courtyard, a framed photo collage on the wall, and so on.

"Let's get a huge rock for the courtyard," one suggested.

"Yeah, and we could get it engraved with our 'arm in arm' group theme from this year," another added.

Everyone agreed, so I started working with my amazing staff team to make it happen. It turns out that ordering a huge several-hundred-pound boulder in China and getting it engraved was much more complicated than I thought. It had to be transported by truck from another province and was set to arrive in late summer of 2013, after the end of their program.

"I'll be sure to send you all a picture of it when it comes in a couple months," I told them in the airport as they left Shanghai back for the US.

Finally, it was the day of the delivery, and I biked over to the facility in the morning to pick out a spot on the courtyard lawn with Gina, one of my program staff. She had coordinated all the logistics with the truck company.

"Gina, it's actually on my heart to dig a little hole and leave something under the rock," I told her.

"Really?" she asked. "What did you have in mind?"

"Well, I put two important things inside this capsule," I said, holding up a clear plastic cylindrical capsule about the size of my thumb, closed up with a cork on the end.

"Is this about Chase?" she asked.

I nodded and went on. "One of the things inside is a folded-up goodbye letter I wrote to Chase several months ago, something he doesn't need to read but I needed to write."

She shifted her feet, looking down and then back up at me. I knew she cared deeply about Chase and about me.

"I also put a small piece of candy inside. See? It's the same kind of gumdrop candy I had in that bowl in my office for the students."

Gina smiled, familiar with my office "rule" that students could only get candy from my bowl if they answered a question from my favorite 1,001 questions book.

I went on. "To me, the candy symbolizes the sweetness God has released over me in this time of closure and pain."

She studied the little plastic capsule, nodding.

"I feel like this is part of the closure process I'm going through." I wiped away a tear as she reached out to hug me.

She ran inside to grab a small shovel, and together, we marked out a good spot on the lawn. As I started digging, my teardrops disappeared into the grass below. This time, it was Gina's hand on my shoulder. She was crying too, as I placed the capsule down into the dirt.

It was done.

I carefully covered up the hole just as the noisy truck arrived, carrying the boulder through the front gate of the property. We craned our necks to get a look at the inscription: "Forever Arm in Arm, 2012–13."

"Perfect!" I told Gina. "Great job arranging this."

It took five local guys from the truck company to heave the huge rock to the ground. Then they started rolling it the fifteen yards or so toward the spot we had prepared for it. It was an amusing spectacle because they kept stopping to take smoke breaks. Cigarettes dangled in their determined lips as they pushed and pushed.

One roll of the boulder, end over end, then another. The sun was shining brightly, another scorching Shanghai summer day. They still had a ways to go, and I remember looking at my watch: 11:06 a.m.

I sucked in my breath.

No way could You be planning this for 11:11 a.m., Lord. No way!

I just smiled and watched as the guys took their sweet time rolling the boulder and muttering to themselves about how heavy it was. It rolled and rolled and was almost there.

The final push came, and it landed with a thud in its new home. I looked down at my wrist: 11:11 a.m.

Of course.

I thought about Chase. His twins had been born, he had proposed to his girlfriend, and I had come to a place in recent months where I felt led to pray for his redemption in the context of his new family. The final divorce papers were set to arrive any day. I looked up to the sky and saw two birds circling. As I reflected on my "11-11" journey with the God of the Universe, I started humming a worship song Chase and I had sung together long ago called "I Cannot Help."

Later that night, I wrote out the lyrics of the song in my journal. They were about being compelled to magnify, glorify, and worship God. Then I wrote the following:

Memories, captured in musical notes and lyrics, float in from
the past,
Bringing tears of pain, tears of joy
How could this be?
How could this be?
How could this be?
I cannot hold back
I have to worship

Thinking of the amazing sweetness that has been released over
these years of pain
Sweetness of God's Spirit
His attentiveness to my cries,
Cries to be known, heard, understood
Cries to understand, cries for everything
So many tears
So many triumphs
Truth emerging, clouded over, then emerging again

I continue to walk in Truth, in the reality of God's heart,
God's kingdom
Even as the outcome I so desperately wanted is now surrendered
and out of my grasp
Surrendered and at His feet
It's not mine to grasp
Not mine to cling to
But... it is mine to call out "Freedom!" in the face of injustice
Freedom in the face of whatever circumstances
Whatever outcome
I walk in freedom. I walk in joy. I walk in hope

I choose abundant life
Life with my Creator. Life in His capable hands
The hands of the One who sees outside of our time
Who declares Truth, and the enemy trembles and scurries
away, terrified
There is no one like our God
He is the great I am
He sees. He redeems. He restores

11–11, *full circle*
Burying the remembrances. Never to be forgotten
Two birds circle, divorce papers crumpled in their mouths, waiting
to land
Waiting for their time to deliver
Signaling one kind of end but also a beginning
Bittersweet messengers of pain and joy
Living Truth reigns
Overcoming all, outside of time

A new season to begin.
Closure. Freedom
A new name, vision…
Restoration.
Waiting here for You
My hands lifted in praise
It is You I love
You I adore
Hallelujah
I cannot hold back
I have to worship

CHAPTER 28

Immersed

The papers came from Chase's lawyer on September 13, 2013, in an email with the ugly words "dissolution of marriage" and "irreconcilable differences."

I hated those words. I hated divorce, yet the sense of closure persisted.

The ministry school in Mozambique, where I planned to be from October through December of 2013, had emailed me a few weeks earlier in response to my application. They said they had prayed over it and sensed it was not yet the right time for me to be in Africa and that I needed to rest after what I had been through. I was shocked by this rejection and was also curious what the Lord was up to. I had been so sure I would be accepted to the program that I had not only already taken the time off work, I even had a house and cat sitter lined up.

During the week I'd received the rejection, a speaker visited our church. He was a young man from Israel named Jacob. Leanna called to tell me about him and the program he ran with his wife, who was a friend of Leanna's and a former member of our church. Their program, Ha'azinu (Hebrew for "listen"), was located in southern Israel and emphasized listening to God, studying scriptures from the Jewish perspective, and walking the literal paths of people from biblical times.

"You know, I can see you going to Israel, Corrie. Not only because of your family connections there but because it would be such a beautiful place for you to rest," Leanna said.

Intrigued, I decided to attend the event the following night. Jacob spoke on a passage from Revelation, and I was fascinated by the Jewish perspectives he brought to the scriptures. He had a sincere and humble demeanor that exuded peace, and he spoke with compelling conviction.

After the event, I introduced myself briefly and asked a bit about the Ha'azinu program. "I have Jewish relatives in Israel," I told him.

"Wonderful." He smiled. A dark brown goatee surrounded his wide grin. "Feel free to follow up with me by email, and my wife and I can share more about it with you. We would love to welcome you to Israel."

I started to correspond with him and his wife, and as I got to know them better, I started to get increasingly excited about the idea of being in Israel. It would be for the first half of what was now shaping up to be a three-month post-divorce sabbatical. I decided to spend the second half of the sabbatical in the US with my family—resting, attending my sister's wedding, and getting all my name-change paperwork done.

I'm going back to my maiden name. So strange but so good too. And God, You set me up! I would have never had the guts to ask my boss for three months off to rest.

In my application for Ha'azinu, I wrote, "I feel God calling me into a season of rest and intimacy with Him after my devastating *and glorious* last three years."

When October finally came, I set off for Israel, a place I'd never been but had heard about through my Jewish grandmother in the US as well as from my Jewish aunts and cousins who lived in Jerusalem and Tel Aviv. For the first two weeks, I would be touring around Israel with them.

The climate there was exactly the same as California's—warm and sunny—and I was surprised by how tropical it felt. I was greeted warmly by my aunts and cousins, who eagerly showed me around the sites, including the Yad Vashem Holocaust Remembrance Center. My heart was continually stirred as I walked through the old city of Jerusalem. I imagined my grandparents living there during the Second World War.

When it was time to start my Ha'azinu program with Jacob, my cousin drove me the ninety minutes from Tel Aviv down to southern Israel. The tiny town was near the Dead Sea and surrounded by desert wilderness. The air seemed still in this area, and everything felt slower in the best possible way. I studied each day along with a small group of other students under Jacob's teaching in his home, and we all took short trips around the small country. The teachings were invigorating, and the accommodations were beautiful and comfortable.

One morning, a few of us got up early and walked out to the edge of a desert cliff to watch the sunrise. Jacob pulled out a tiny portable camping stove and proceeded to boil water then combined fragrant coffee grounds and fresh cardamom. It was the best Turkish coffee I'd ever tasted. I remember him looking off at the distant horizon where brilliant gold and orange rays were emerging.

"You know, God took His people here into the wilderness not to punish them but to teach them." He took a sip of coffee from his thermos then continued.

"He wanted to quiet them down to hear His voice and train them to walk with Him. He took them here because He wanted to draw near to them."

"It is exceptionally quiet here," I replied. "Deeply quiet, like in my soul. Being here makes me want to slow everything down."

Jacob smiled. "Yes, Corrianah. That's how we are meant to live. Much more slowly."

Everyone in Israel called me Corrianah, which was a new name I had recently sensed God calling me, like how I was known in heavenly realms. When I asked God what it meant, I heard: "*Completely submitted to Me.*" I remembered when God declared new names for people in the Bible— like Abraham, Sarah, and Israel, who had previously been Abram, Sarai, and Jacob—He was calling them into a new level of faith.

During my days in southern Israel, I walked the wilderness trails with the beauty of this new name. I felt transported into the spiritual realm where I was safe and free and where all things were lovely, so lovely, where there was no pain, no darkness, and no confusion; where there was radiant joy and color and stillness. No anxiety, no accusation, no discouragement. No Noise. My conversations with God in this place became whimsical and childlike.

Where are we going to play today, God?

I would walk through the market with Him, picking out dates, avocados, pears, pita bread, and hummus. I would marvel at spectacular tropical pink flowers and towering stalks of white blooms.

Oh, the beauty of the heavenly spiritual realm. I'd seen glimpses of it in this tropical desert place and in the underwater world when I was scuba diving in the Philippines. I longed for that beauty; the beauty we were created for of uninterrupted communion with God. I pondered how we, as humans, are constantly in a state of mourning, not made for a broken world. Yet we live here and we cope, day by day. We were made for the other place, and we all long for home, for things to be set right again.

As I thought back to my three years of crying out for my husband, I realized I was also crying out for all broken things in this seen world to be healed and made whole again. Before my crisis, I wasn't in tune with the brokenness around me. Now I saw it, and now I felt the pulse of pain in the land, screaming to be redeemed. I could hear that scream in my own scream.

Oh Lord, come and set things right again.

Two major questions were still weighing on me as I walked with God:

Why did Chase's eyes open and then close again when he came back for that month during the summer of 2011?

Why couldn't he cross the bridge he mentioned in that final counseling session and reconcile with me?

I took time to journal daily and kept walking the sandy trails to pray. It got to be my second to last day in Israel, and I still didn't have clarity. I walked into my bedroom frustrated, taking off my shoes after a long prayer walk where I heard nothing but silence.

God, I really want answers to those questions. I've been asking You for weeks.

Then I heard it, as clearly as I'd ever heard anything from God.

Are you done?

Done what? I asked, genuinely perplexed.

Done trying to control your own healing process?

I stopped short.

Oh, wow. I have definitely been doing that.

I flopped onto my bed and laid on my back, arms stretched open.

Yes, God, I'm done. I'm done.

What happened next I can best describe as a "two-minute download" of insights and whispers from God that poured in to answer my questions.

The reconciliation period was a gift, I heard, tearing up as I remembered the beautiful sound of "I'm sorry" and "I love you" from Chase's lips.

The last counseling session was also a gift, I heard. I remembered the exhilaration of putting my whole heart out there in the letter I'd read aloud to Chase in front of Karim a year and a half earlier. I also remembered the strange feeling of bumping against what felt like an invisible wall between us.

Lastly, I heard: ***Corrie, you did everything you could. It's time to say goodbye to Chase.***

I was balling then, heaving with sobs as I felt the release deep in my soul. The time for contending for the marriage was over.

I'm Yours, God. I'm completely Yours. Thank You.

My time in Israel helped me solidify that though God's heart was for the reconciliation of my marriage, the redemption He had for me was taking a different form than I had originally hoped. Chase, in his free will, had walked away. The journey toward my hoped-for outcome had a deeper purpose.

My life had been transformed during these three years. My heart was healing, my sense of my calling was sharpened, and my boldness was off the charts. The fearful and condemning Noise in my life was continually muted by God's voice. I was free from my fixation on Chase, and my new fixation was on living the life God created me to live.

I sat upright on the bed with thoughts moving to my flight, which was leaving for the US the next day. I sensed a stirring to do something to commemorate this moment of my life, and an idea dropped into my mind. I called my Israeli aunt Naomi.

"Auntie, tomorrow, before you take me to the airport, can you drive me to the Mediterranean Sea? I haven't been in it yet."

In Jacob's teaching and in our sightseeing, we had learned about the traditional Jewish "mikvah"—a pool of water for ritual purification and the origin of the Christian practice of baptism. I had also been struck by a quote from Pastor Kent Carlson my mom had sent during the first year of my crisis.

"Hope is not tied to the preferred end to our suffering. Hope is being immersed in a reality that is greater than our suffering."

Immersed.

Early the next morning, we arrived at the shore of an empty beach facing an endless expanse of radiant turquoise. The waves were small, and I waded out easily past the breakers, goose bumps covering my legs in the cool water. My aunt waited silently on the shore.

"I'll just be a minute," I told her.

I pushed my toes down into the sand as I lifted off and dove head first into the sea, kicking my legs calmly underwater until my body temperature adjusted. I swam further out for a minute or two until I felt I was in my own space with my Creator.

Here I am, God.

I remembered one needed to be completely naked in a traditional Jewish *mikvah*.

Okay, here we go. I'm all in with You, God.

I carefully peeled off my swimsuit, took a deep breath, and plunged under the water. I stretched out my limbs, suspended for a few moments, completely immersed with the God of the Universe.

Here I am, God.
I am Yours.

Darkness was around me
A black abyss
Then pinpricks of light
Beautiful beams, streaming through
Patches to bathe in
Soaking
Changing
Learning to see that light

Catching glimpse after glimpse of Your world
The Spirit realm
A place of beauty, redemption, wholeness
I taste it, feel it, swim in it
Your Kingdom
Here
I'm here
Surrounded by light
I see it!
It's You!

Contending for years was about...
Yes, I see it
Dipping in, again and again
Immersed in hope
Refreshed, healed, moved to tears that flow in joy,
Flow in sadness, flow in longing

My clinging fingers loosen their grasp
On outcome
Longed for, hoped for
My idol, blanket, security
Outcome was my entry point
Now I watch it float away
The fuel, driving me for so long…
To chase the light, chase the victory

I see a new story
Brilliant, unfolding
The tapestry flips
And just like that
Reveals the beauty

Well done, *I feel You say*
You're always welcome here

As my face burst out of the water, my heart was singing and my mind was still.

Thank You, Lord.

Just then, I noticed a few other swimmers surprisingly nearby, and I rushed to put my suit back on. I waved to my aunt on shore, and she waved back. Swimming forward, my feet found the sandy sea floor. Then, step by step, I walked through the stillness of the water back to the beach.

I am the Lord; that is my name! I will not yield my glory to another or my praise to idols. See, the former things have taken place, and new things I declare…

—Isaiah 42:8–9a[1]

Epilogue

After the divorce was finalized in September of 2013, I stayed in China for an additional four years before moving back to the US to get a master's in dispute resolution. During the third year of my program, when I had finally embraced the idea that singleness could still be an amazing path in life, I met an incredible man who was just as intent as I was to see God's kingdom come on Earth as it is in heaven.

His name was John Napier, and we recognized immediately we were running in the same direction. I married him ten months later, and as fellow peace-makers and bridge-builders, we started a consultancy and mediation practice together in Virginia Beach, Virginia. We are serving each other, serving God, serving the community, and absolutely thriving. I could not be more grateful.

When I think about my life now and what I want for my future, a simple picture comes to mind. It's not about ideal circumstances or outcomes, though of course those can be good. It's a picture of my hand in God's hand, walking through life together, knowing Him intimately, hearing and responding to His voice.

Experiencing a love bigger and stronger than the brokenness and pain of the world. Entering a secret place with Him and tapping into a spiritual realm that is, in fact, a taste of my true home, His kingdom come now, eternal life now, a supernatural place of smoothness and comfort, better than the smoothness and comfort of circumstances.

I can't wait to one day enter it fully.

Next Steps

If you would like to reach out to Corrie Napier or explore the ideas from *Fierce Hope*, feel free to visit **www.CorrieNapier. com**, where you will find practical resources to fuel your next steps.

Acknowledgments

I am compelled to first acknowledge my Creator—my Father, my Friend, and the Lover of my soul. You get all the credit, all the glory, all the honor, and all the praise. I thank You for revealing Yourself to me, for putting a new song in my mouth, and for putting my feet on a solid rock. May all who read this see, experience, and know You are God.

John, my beloved husband, life partner, and best friend, how did I get you? I'm in awe of the confident, grounded man you are and how in tune you are with me and with the Lord. Thank you for the endless processing, editing, glasses of water, and, most of all, encouragement.

Michael and Debi, my incredible parents, you have been my unwavering supporters and champions from my first day of life. God used your wisdom, encouragement, prayers, and physical presence during the pain years to help me understand my value and what it feels like to be truly and sacrificially loved. I am eternally grateful.

Azin, you were and are a gift from God. Thank you for creating a safe place for years to help me feel seen, make sense of internal chaos, and have the courage to tolerate such prolonged uncertainty and even thrive in the midst of it. Your wisdom, perspective, and word pictures remain treasures to me.

Nina and Chris, thank you for speaking this out when you prayed for me in the fall of 2022: "Corrie, I sense God wants to birth something through you before a baby. I hear him saying 'Birth *that*. Birth *that*.'" Well, here it is. The book baby has been born, glory to God.

To my Shanghai friends, who were my family before, during, and after the pain years, I'm eternally grateful to God for how you walked with me, listened to me, fed me (literally), prayed with me, and reminded me of my value. A very special shout out to Judi for teaching me to live by assignment and for fiercely following through on yours.

To all my friends and family around the world who prayed for me and even fasted with me during the pain years, thank you for being with me in spirit, holding my arms up, and sending me scriptures, dreams, songs, visions, and encouraging words.

To an inspirational author, Johnny Savage, thank you for demonstrating this "writing a book thing" could be done. When I asked you how you did it, you simply said, "Two words: Call Eric." I'm so glad I did.

To the team at Manuscripts LLC, thank you for providing a platform to bring my book to life. Eric Koester, you were the first to recognize and call out the "fierce" spark in me and my story. Thank you for getting me "nervited." Kehkashan Khalid, your enthusiasm, excellent feedback, and accountability kept me focused and motivated during the grueling revisions stage. Katie Sigler, Tatiana Obey, George Thorne, Angela Ivey, Shanna Heath, and Clayton Bohle also deserve special thanks for investing in me, keeping me on track, and helping me trust the process.

Finally, thanks to my incredible launch team! This generous community of people believed in me so fervently they preordered their copies of *Fierce Hope* and helped make its publishing possible. Many of you gave feedback on early chapter drafts as well as on the book title and cover. Special thanks to Lisa Söderlund, who pored over my entire manuscript with a loving, fine-toothed comb, as well as to Nurit Nitzan, whose loving ear and input helped crystallize the themes in this book. I am still blown away by the sheer number of people who came out of the woodwork to support me. You are listed here in alphabetical order by last name.

Jenieva Abner
Cigdem Alan
Pamela Angleman
Annie and Chris Avery
Lindsay and Rich Barton
Malika and Paul Begin
Jennifer Brown
Emily Brown
Andrew and Esther Brumme
Elizabeth Crandall Butcher
Ross and Hannah Byrd
Fiona Li and Peter Chin
Tyler Clark
La Shonda Coleman

Kristy and Chris Collins
Susan Collins
Danny and Jill Coyle
Sally Eliza Cranham
Caroline and Blake Dozier
Mary Drummond
Brittany and Pat Dunn
Maria English
Barbara and Brian Englund
Susan and Rick Farmar
Heather and Matt Fischer
Mary and Freddie Fletcher
Laurie and Drew Fralick
Jim and Joline Gash

Michael and Joy Goffman
Thomas Griffin IV
Kara and Hunter Hanger
Katherine Hansen
Mary Jo Hardman
Cathy and Phil Harris
Diane Harris
Dana and Jason Hinojosa
Harriett and Dave Hinton
Annie Lu and Eddie Hsu
Justina Huang
Kelly and Robbie Hughes
Sarah and Dave Hummel
Abby and Skyler Isch
Janet James
Nancy Jenster
Dr. Amanda Jones
Tracy and John Kaptan
Meg and Scott Kelsey
Janet Kerr
Sophie Kessler
Jennifer and Phil Kinney
Lindsey Kirchhoff
William and Linda Knorr
Eric Koester
Judi and Bob Kohlbacher
Lani and Brian Koontz
Brian Korchin
Creedance Kresch
Joshua and Coco Lange
Diana Lee
Yetong Li

Nick and Sonia Liao
Kwan Lieu
MK and David Lim
Brett and Jessica Lovellette
Celeste Luce
Bixia Luo
Jean Lyu
Jay and Holly McCabe
Jaclyn and Jason McClure
Jeffrey McMahan
Connie and Bruce Meyer
Krissy and Brian Millar
Emily Milnes
Lindsay and Ray Mollett
Stacy Montgomery
Phillip Moran
Jen and Patrick Muscenti
Sandy and Martha Napier
David and Courtney Napier
Azin and Shelly Nasseri
Brian and Dina Newman
Heather and Brandon Newmyer
Drs. Ulrike and Klaus Niehaus
Alan Palmer
Kyle Pang
Ryan and Tatjana Pearce
Kaylee and John Powers
Jing Qin
Taryn and Buddy Raschdorf
Abigail and Sean Reilly

Jim and Kim Richardson
Megan Riggs
Tarin Riley
Caitlin Robertson
Jessica Rockey
Diane Samandi
David Santiago-Diaz
Claire Shallow
Hope Sherman
Nichole and Robert Skelton
Jim and Linda Slattery
Kristina and Timon Smith
Ethan Smith
Cecilia So
Lisa Söderlund and John Atkins
Nina Sprenger
David and Hannah Spring
Emily and Aris Stavrianos
Angelique and Greg Stevens
Rebecca and Mark Stevenson
Cynthia Hinojosa and Sidney Tassin

Edward and Shirley Talen
Nadine Tapia
Shirley Terry
Pauline Thg
Suzana Tsai
Kevin and Wanda Turpin
Dale and Kristine Vander Wall
Helen Vander Wall
Laury Vander Wall
Joel and Kellie Vaughan
Pam and Earl Wiersma
N. Wong
Suzie Wratten
Kristin and Christopher Wratten
Michael and Debi Zacharia
Jordan Zacharia
Tyler and Katie Zacharia
OnNi Zacharia
Jon Zemke

Sponsors

To the sponsors of this book, who went above and beyond in generosity, thank you for being champions of *Fierce Hope*! I am truly humbled by your special outpouring of love and support.

Silver Sponsors
Michael and Debi Zacharia
Sandy and Martha Napier

Bronze Sponsors
Malika and Paul Begin
Kara and Hunter Hanger

Notes

AUTHOR'S NOTE

1. 2 Corinthians 1:3–4 (NIV).
2. Graham Cooke, "Live Brilliantly," Brilliant Perspectives, Brilliant, accessed April 8, 2024, www.brilliantperspectives.com.
3. Jeremiah 18: 1–2 (NIV).
4. Genesis 28:12–19 (NIV).
5. Genesis 37:7 (NIV).
6. John 16:13 (NIV).
7. Romans 8:14–15 (NIV).

CHAPTER 2—ENCOUNTERING GOD

1. Psalm 40:1–3a, 4, 9a, 11, 12b, 13a, 17a (NIV).

CHAPTER 5—THE PAIN BEGINS

1. Psalm 46:1–4, 10–11 (NIV).

CHAPTER 6—THE PREPARATION

1. Psalm 46:1–3, 10 (NIV).
2. Leviticus 23:24b (NIV).
3. Joshua 6:5 (NIV).
4. Psalm 40:9a (NIV).

5. 2 Corinthians 9:8, 11 (NIV).

CHAPTER 7—THE DEAD RISE
1. Psalm 42:1–3a, 5 (NIV).

CHAPTER 12—THE PRAYER WARRIOR
1. 1 Peter 5:6–9a, 10 (NIV).
2. 2 Corinthians 10:3–5 (NIV).

CHAPTER 14—BUT EVEN IF HE DOES NOT
1. Daniel 3:13–18 (NIV).

CHAPTER 16—JAZZ
1. Psalm 46:1–3 (NIV).

CHAPTER 20—NATASHA BEDINGFIELD
1. Zephaniah 3:17 (ESV).

CHAPTER 25—FUNERAL IN THE FOREST
1. Philippians 4:11b (NIV).
2. Hannah Hurnard, *Hinds' Feet on High Places* (Blacksburg, Virginia: Wilder Publications, Inc., 2010), 43.

CHAPTER 28—IMMERSED
1. Isaiah 42:8–9a (NIV).

Made in the USA
Middletown, DE
08 September 2024

60611698R00169